W9-AHK-434

VIOLENCE

WITHDRAWN
WELLESLEY FREE LIBRARY

Also by Raymond B. Flannery Jr., Ph.D., FAPM

Becoming Stress-resistant through the Project SMART Program

Posttraumatic Stress Disorder: The Victim's Guide to Healing and Recovery

Violence in the Workplace

The Assaulted Staff Action Program (ASAP):
Coping with the Psychological Aftermath of Violence

Violence in America: Coping with Drugs, Distressed Families,
Inadequate Schooling, and Acts of Hate

Preventing Youth Violence: A Guide for Parents, Teachers, and Counselors

The Violent Person: Professional Risk Management Strategies for Safety and Care

VIOLENCE

Why People Do Bad Things,

with Strategies to Reduce that Risk

Raymond B. Flannery Jr., Ph.D., FAPM

2016

AMHF
AMERICAN
MENTAL
HEALTH
FOUNDATION
BOOKS

American Mental Health Foundation Inc
128 Second Place Garden Suite
Brooklyn New York 11231-4102

Copyright © 2016 by Raymond B. Flannery Jr.

All rights reserved. No part of this book may be reproduced,
stored in a retrieval system, or transmitted in any form
or by any means, electronic, mechanical, photocopying,
recording, or otherwise, without the written permission of
The American Mental Health Foundation Inc
and American Mental Health Foundation Books.

Printed in the United States of America

americanmentalhealthfoundation.org

Library of Congress Cataloging-in-Publication Data

Names: Flannery, Raymond B., author.
Title: Violence : why people do bad things
with strategies to reduce that
risk / Raymond B. Flannery, Ph.D., FAPM.
Description: New York : American Mental
Health Foundation Books, 2016.
Identifiers: LCCN 2015036407| ISBN 9781590565247
(hardcover : alk. paper) |
ISBN 9781590565377 (pbk. : alk. paper) |
ISBN 9781590565384 (ebook)
Subjects: LCSH: Violence. | Violence—Prevention.
Classification: LCC HM1116 .F585 2016 | DDC 303.6—dc23
LC record available at http://lccn.loc.gov/2015036407

For BOSTON STRONG, especially
        Krystel Cambell
        Officer Sean Collier
        Lingzi Lu
        Martin Richards
        Officer Dennis Simmonds
whose lives were taken and the 264 other men,
women, and children who were wounded in the
Boston Marathon terrorist bombings on
        April 15, 2013

WELLESLEY FREE LIBRARY
WELLESLEY, MASS. 02482

Contents

Publisher's Foreword

As the present book is issued, The American Mental Health Foundation reaches upward and grows toward 100 years of philanthropic work. AMHF is dedicated to the welfare of people suffering from emotional problems, with a focus on at-risk youth, individuals of any age with special needs, and elders. Historically, AMHF devoted its efforts to bettering quality of treatment and developing more effective methods, making all of this available to lower-income wage earners. Today, the mission of AMHF lies in three areas: research, publishing, and educational seminars/Webinars.

Conceived as one of the first nonprofit foundations of its kind, AMHF has been a pioneering force in research and advocacy. Its major therapeutic advances and improved training methods are described in several publications: the three-part series The Search for the Future. Two of these books are available on the AMHF Web site under the titles *The Challenge for Group Psychotherapy* (volume 1) and *The Challenge for Psychoanalysis and Psychotherapy: Solutions for the Future* (volume 2). Portions of these books are also reprinted on the AMHF Web site in French and German. Volume 3, originally issued in 2000, is available from AMHF Books in traditional and e-book formats: *Crucial Choices—Crucial Changes: The Resurrection of Psychotherapy.*

AMHF Books has been an exciting venture since it was launched in late 2009. In addition to *Crucial Choices—Crucial Changes,* it includes seven other titles by Dr. Raymond B. Flannery Jr., one of the world's foremost experts on posttraumatic stress disorder (PTSD); four classic books (two reissued, two posthumously published) by Erich Fromm; *Live Your Dreams, Change the World: The Psychology of Personal Fulfillment for Women* by Drs. Joanne H. Gavin, James Campbell Quick, and David J. Gavin; and by Dr. Henry Kellerman, an additional four: *Group Psychotherapy and Personality; Personality: How It Forms; Anatomy of Delusion;* and *There's No Handle on My Door: Stories of Patients in Mental Hospitals.*

The present book is issued to observe the quarter-century of significant research on psychological trauma, posttraumatic stress disorder, and their impact on victims of all sorts. *Violence: Why People Do Bad Things, with Strategies to Reduce that Risk* probes the subject through key chapters—revised as necessary (and there were few revisions based on new research) to bring the subject up to the minute—of Dr. Raymond B. Flannery's other groundbreaking books. Flannery has been studying psychological trauma and posttraumatic stress disorder before the term became widely known and accepted. His work forms one of the reasons PTSD is now part of the lexicon. He designed and fielded the Assaulted Staff Action Program (ASAP), a voluntary, peer-help, crisis-intervention program for employee victims of violence. For twenty-five years, he has overseen the development of this program, now including 2,100 ASAP team members on 45 teams in 9 states that have responded to the needs of more than 8,000 staff victims. This book is part of the AMHF mission to help troubled individuals and victims of violence, as well as to enlighten the public by identifying the warning signs and show what can be done. In short, this book is published to save lives.

* * *

The costs of research, organizing seminars and Webinars, and disseminating the findings in fulfillment of the mission of AMHF are high. All donations, made via PayPal on the foundation Web site, or posted to the address listed on the copyright page of this book, constitute a meaningful contribution to the public good. If your commitment is deeper, consider partnering with AMHF in the form of a legacy bequest, so that the foundation would continue to serve society for another 100 years. We thank you for your interest in the present book and for helping AMHF build a more compassionate society. Please discover our work in greater detail on the Web site:

americanmentalhealthfoundation.org

Preface

We live in troubled times. The various forms of media report on terrorist acts, murders, rapes, robberies, vicious assaults, arson, embezzlements and the like on a daily basis. Even though violence has decreased in the past decade, much remains to be done and the average citizen at times still feels ill-at-ease and concerned for the safety of self and loved ones. Violence teaches all of us how tenuous our links are to Mother Earth. The seriousness of this problem has led to continued research into the nature of violence and the development of risk management strategies to reduce this risk.

In the mid-1980s and early 1990s, the United States military and the Women's Movement drew attention to the victims of violent acts, especially in combat and rape. Medicine and behavioral science followed suit, expanded research on violence to include victims, began to evaluate the physical and psychological impact of violence on victims. Psychological trauma and posttraumatic stress disorder (PTSD) were identified as serious and costly aspects of violence.

On this roughly twenty-fifth anniversary of the emergence of psychological trauma and PTSD as important components in the study of violence, Evander Lomke of The American Mental Health Foundation approached me about developing a book on the subject and its impact on victims, drawn from chapters in my earlier books, which would be geared toward the general reader. This volume is in response to that request.

My book is written for this audience, including high-school and college students as well as first-responders who want a concise yet comprehensive overview of an issue that affects society on a daily basis.

Part 1 reviews the extent and frequency of violent acts that cause such mayhem, and focuses as well on the causes for such violence and its impact on victims. Part 2 reviews the various risk management strategies that may be employed to reduce the risk of such violence. Although medicine and the behavioral sciences cannot predict violence with one-hundred percent accuracy, there are still steps that can be implemented to reduce the risk and contain the impact in its aftermath. The risk management strategies include procedures for reducing risk in the community, in the workplace, and among violent youth. The last two chapters outline strategies to treat victims in the aftermath of violent incidents both in the longer term and in its immediate aftermath.

As noted, countless individuals are concerned about violence but often do not understand its roots or how to reduce the risk to ensure safety. My hope is that this book begins to address this need.

* * *

An author's intellectual roots are many and diverse. I would like to thank my patients and students over the years who have taught me much about violence and victimization, the several members of the Assaulted Staff Action Program teams, and the science community that continues to unravel the unknowns of violence. A word of special thanks to my editor at The American Mental Health Foundation, its executive director Evander Lomke, and to my wife Georgina, reference librarian par excellence, critical thinker, and soulmate.

Raymond B. Flannery Jr., Ph.D., FAPM
Summer, 2015

Author's Note and Editorial Method

Forms of inquiry into the causes, treatment, and risk reduction strategies are constantly being upgraded and the latest research findings should be considered. The present chapters are updated as of summer, 2015. General guidelines and principles are presented here but, since violence cannot be predicted with 100 percent accuracy, this book is not intended as a substitute for the advice and counsel of policing personnel, lawyers, and/or professional counselors who may be necessary in specific situations. Raise any questions that you may have with these various professionals and always weigh and follow their advice first.

With respect to psychological trauma and posttraumatic stress disorder, medicines and other forms of treatment are also constantly being upgraded and improved. This book is not intended to provide therapy and is not a substitute for the advice of your physician or professional counselor. Raise any questions that you may have with them and always follow the advice of your physician or counselor. *First.*

* * *

The end of each chapter notes the book from which the chapter text was taken. Citations in the chapter text may be found in the Readings List in the back of each book.

* * *

All of the examples in this book are based on real events that have impacted individuals. In some cases the examples are those of one person, in others they are based on composites of impacted individuals. To the extent possible, identifying information has been omitted to preserve anonymity.

PART ONE

Violence:
Its Nature and Impact

ONE

It's the Nature of the Times: Cultural Factors in Violence

Cain rose up against his brother Abel and killed him.
—GENESIS 4:8

We are all in the same boat, in a stormy sea. . . .
—G. K. CHESTERTON

Dateline: San Francisco, California. July 1, 1993.
The apartment was empty. Eviction notices were posted. The
sense of failure seared one's soul. A moment of shattered glass also
seared the soul of ten-month-old Catherine. . . .
    The dream had begun earnestly enough ten years before. The
would-be speculator had the California dream of making his for-
tune in real estate, and the attorneys of one of the city's best law
firms had helped him broker his first deal for mobile trailer parks
in Indiana and Kentucky. The world was his for the taking.
    A decade of real estate deals attempted and failed had passed,
including three recent forays in Las Vegas. The downward spi-
ral had been slow and continuous, and a recent recession had
brought financial ruin. Charges of fraud by former inves-
tors. Unpaid taxes. Unpaid rent. Nine dollars in his checking
account precluded his declaring personal bankruptcy.
    On this pleasant Thursday afternoon, the failed speculator,
dressed in suit and tie, packed his briefcase with two nine-
millimeter semiautomatic pistols, a forty-five caliber automatic

handgun, several rounds of ammunition. Included also were his four-page letter with its charges of being "raped" by advisors and the names of the fifty people who had to pay for this bad advice.

Arriving in the business district, this neat, polite, fifty-five-year-old man, who had abhorred violence all his life, quietly rode the elevator to the thirty-fourth floor, the law offices of the firm that had helped him get his start. When the doors opened, he was calm and expressionless as he turned to the right, walked to a glass-enclosed disposition room, and opened fire. Catherine's mother was one of the first to die in the shattered glass. Another was the law firm's senior partner.

He marched down to the thirty-third floor where he met a young married couple. Inseparable since college, they would now be inseparable in death. The husband shielded his wife and was fatally wounded.

The thirty-second floor.
The thirty-first floor.
The thirtieth floor.

So it went until, in the stairwell of the twenty-ninth floor, the gunman shot himself to death as the police charged toward him.

Amid the anguished echoes of the first-floor atrium that now served as a field hospital, the toll was assessed: eight dead, six wounded, and hundreds terrified and grieving.

For fifteen long, terrifying, and ugly minutes, the world had been his for the taking. The sense of failure seared one's soul.

The United States is a violent country. Episodes of violent crime, like this one in San Francisco, are not exceptions to the rule. Indeed, comparative statistics among nations (Dobrin, Wiersema, Loftin, and McDowall, 1996) indicate that the United States outranks most other nations of the industrial world in violent crimes like assault, rape, and robbery. In the category of murder, we are far and away the most violent industrialized nation on earth. Consider the following informal national survey of homicides drawn at random.

- Waterville, Maine—Two elderly nuns are murdered in their convent by a thirty-seven-year-old male.
- Boston, Massachusetts—A sixty-one-year-old free-lance photographer sells photos to a newspaper of a fatal accident

scene. Ten days later he is charged with running over one of the victims.

- New York, New York—A twenty-seven-year-old female health aide beats two elderly women to death for their money.
- Toledo, Ohio—A fifteen-year-old boy kills his sixty-two-year-old foster mother with a hatchet and sets her on fire because she would not allow him to keep a stray dog.
- Chicago, Illinois—A young, pregnant mother of three is murdered by her former boyfriend, who extracts the fetus from the deceased mother to take as his own child.
- York, Nebraska—A fifty-seven-year-old woman is sexually assaulted, and then her attacker runs over her in a car, shortly before Christmas.
- Salt Lake City, Utah—A ninth-grade male student hijacks a school bus, shoots the driver, and commits suicide.
- Portland, Oregon—A ten-year-old boy pleads guilty to manslaughter in the death of his five-year-old sister, who would not go to her room as he directed.

This prohibitive murder rate, in addition to the other unacceptably high levels of violent crime, is creating a nation of anxious and demoralized citizens who feel angry at being captives of this violence and at being helpless to stop it.

Many live in houses with extra locks on the doors and a perimeter security system around their homes, similar antitheft devices on their vehicles, and an attack dog for company. They go to work furtively to avoid being mugged in transit and enter worksites that require special-issue surveillance cards to gain access. Even within the building they have to lock up personal possessions to avoid theft. At home again in the evening, the televised news offers no respite. A plane is downed by a terrorist on a routine flight. A mother calmly drowns her young children because she did not like them. Should one go for a walk in the evening air to calm down? Few are the souls that would venture forth in their neighborhoods after dark. Better to wait until daylight when you might be able to escape or at least obtain a description of your assailant. They may be told that crime is decreasing, but it does not make them any less anxious. In some ways, they have become prisoners of affluence.

How has it come to this? What are we to make of any of these acts of violence? How are we to understand the massacre in the San Francisco office tower or the mother who destroys her own children? Are these assailants out of their minds? Are they on drugs? Are they hopeless victims of some social ill? More importantly, can we do anything to stop this national crime spree or are we helpless in the face of this madness?

We ask ourselves these questions because violent crime is everywhere. Rural. Urban. Male. Female. Young. Old. All races. All ethnic groups. All religions. Anyone can be a victim. No one is exempt and no one is safe. Violence in America has become a national public health problem of epidemic proportion.

This book is written to help us better understand the current crisis in violence and what we can do to contain and curtail it. We will examine the latest findings in medicine and the behavioral sciences to help us answer the questions that we have raised in order that we can make some sense of this apparent chaos. We shall use this information to outline specific coping strategies that can be employed by individuals, families, and communities to reduce the risk of violence.

Toward these ends, this first chapter provides us with an overview of America's current culture of violence. We begin by examining the nature and extent of violence in America during the past thirty-five years. Then, we shall review the emergence of the postindustrial state, the cultural context that has been evolving during this same thirty-five-year period. Finally, we look at the impact of the postindustrial state on the basic societal institutions of business, government, the family, school, and religion to see if there are cultural risk factors that may suggest links between the emergence of the postindustrial state and the sharp increases in crime that we are about to review.

Although this topic is difficult, the message of this book is one of hope. We are not helpless in the face of violence. We can reduce this needless human suffering. In this spirit, let us begin our inquiry into the nature of violence.

THE NATURE OF VIOLENCE IN AMERICA

Crimes and Criminals: An Overview

Since there are many apparent causes of violent crime, it should not surprise us that there are many differing technical definitions, methods of measurement, and systems for recording incidents, and we will consider these viewpoints in subsequent chapters, but we need clear, basic, general definitions to guide us. We shall define violence as the intentional use of physical force to injure or abuse another, and crime as the commission of an act forbidden by public law. Not all violence is criminal (e.g., self-defense) and not all crime is violent (e.g., fraud and embezzlement), but commonly they overlap (e.g., armed robbery). With these basic definitions let us begin to examine the present nature of violent crime in our country.

Types of Assailants. There has been enough research over the years to identify basic groupings of assailants, and these are noted in Table 1. Some assailants are ordinary citizens. Overcome with anger, fear, jealousy, and greed, they usually commit crimes on impulse (actions without thought) and are truly sorry for these acts within a short period of time. Most never commit a second crime, and the courts deal with these matters in the form of a lesser fine and probation. Medically ill people form the second type of potential assailants. These are persons with disorders such as serious mental illness or pathological intoxication that may lead them

Table 1. Types of Criminals

Average Citizens
Medically Ill Persons
Domestic Batterers
Disgruntled Employees
Juvenile Delinquents
Career Criminals

to violent outbursts. Depending on the circumstances, these persons may not be held accountable for their crimes. Domestic batterers form a third group. Batterers are usually entitled males who have a past history of being victimized by others, who have a current substance abuse problem, and who feel entitled to treat their spouses and children as their personal property. Disgruntled employees form the next grouping. These are often socially isolated persons with problems of substance abuse and access to weapons. Their jobs mean everything to them so that the threat of job loss provokes violence in some.

The last two categories of assailants are juvenile delinquents and career criminals. These two groups contain many repeat offenders and are responsible for the majority of criminal offenses.

Delinquents are young antisocial individuals. They are aggressive with people and with animals, and are often physically cruel to both. They may destroy property, set fires, and steal the belongings of others. They often stay out late at night and are truant from school. Without intervention to curtail this antisocial lifestyle, they often mature into career criminals. The failure to conform to social norms continues. Aggressive and deceitful behavior continues, and they learn the skills necessary to commit the most heinous of acts. They continue to repeat these acts over many years because of the thrill of the chase, the monetary rewards, and increases in power and enhanced self-esteem among their criminal peers.

Since delinquents and career criminals are frequently incarcerated, there have been continuous opportunities to study various aspects of their lives. From 1917 to 1976, students of criminology have conducted ten major studies. Two were of adult criminals by psychiatrist Dr. Sheldon Glueck and his wife Eleanor, a social worker. One study assessed male criminals (1939) and the other, female assailants (1934). There were also eight major studies of juvenile delinquents and these are listed in Table 2. (The references for all of these scientific studies are included in Appendix A for the interested reader.)

These ten studies provide us with an offender sample of 10,800 persons. Included are both genders, all races, all creeds, all ethnic groups, and representatives from a variety of geographical locations in our country. These studies span a fifty-year period, and the findings are remarkably consistent, an important scientific outcome in its own right.

These offenders came from *broken homes* marred by untimely death, divorce, desertion, separation, foster home placement, and unhappy marriages. *Disrupted family lives* were common and included constant family quarreling, domestic abuse of parents and children, alcoholism, gambling, and profound social isolation. *Inadequate parenting* was the norm with inadequate limit setting by adults, erratic punishment, little parental affection, and general emotional neglect. *Inadequate schooling* was also common

Table 2. Studies of Juvenile Delinquents

Study	Number of Subjects	Gender	Major Years of Study	Geographical Location
S. and E. Glueck (1940)	1000	M	1920s	MA
S. and E. Glueck (1950)	499	M	1940s	MA
McCord, McCord, and Zola (1959)	650	M	1940s	MA
Konopk (1966)	181	F	1950s	MN
Robins (1966)	524	M/F	1950s	MO
Wolfgang, Figlio, and Selin (1972)	3481	M	1950s	PA
Ahlstrom and Havighurst (1971)	400	M	1960s	MO
Tracy, Wolfgang, and Figlio (1990)	4315	M	1970s	PA

with fundamental scholastic and behavioral problems and feelings of academic inferiority.

These characteristics represent many of the biological, sociological, and psychological risk factors that we are to consider, but for our purposes in this chapter, these findings also represent a breakdown in community. The network of stable family life, consistent schooling, and supportive services from other adults in the community was not a part of the lives of these offenders, and it is reasonable to assume that this absence of community may have contributed, at least in part, to their violent lifestyle. We shall return to this theme later in the chapter.

Types of Violence and Their Measurement. The types of crimes committed by these assailants are presented in Table 3 and represent the major types of offenses reported in the Federal Bureau of Investigation's (FBI) Uniform Crime Report (UCR). These crimes are known to all of us. Type I offenses are usually the most serious in terms of human suffering, medical expense, sick leave and disability claims, and lost productivity. Type II offenses are the remaining serious categories of criminal acts that people continually inflict on each other. As you can see from the types of crimes listed, as a country we are clearly having problems living together as a community.

Crime is basically measured in two ways. The first is the FBI UCR, which counts crime reported by individuals and businesses. It counts every separate crime it is informed of and is more accurate for the major crimes or Type I offenses. The second common database is the Bureau of the Census' National Crime Victimization Survey (NCVS). The NCVS counts only personal and household victimizations and relies on the victim's memory, but is generally more accurate for the lesser or Type II offenses. These surveys exclude fraud, drug, white-collar, and victimless crimes.

Obtaining an accurate report of these various offenses, however, is not without its difficulties. In addition to the two differing databases, there are other measurement issues. Some victims do not realize that they are victims and do not report the crime: for example, victims of date rape on campus. Some feel that reporting a crime will be of little use in seeking redress. Still others fear

Table 3. FBI Uniform Crime Report: Types of Offenses

Type I Offenses:
Criminal Homicide
Forcible Rape
Robbery
Aggravated Assault
Burglary
Larceny
Auto Theft
Arson

Type II Offenses:
Other Assaults
Forgery and Counterfeiting
Fraud
Embezzlement
Stolen Property (buying, receiving, possession)
Vandalism
Weapons (carrying, possession)
Prostitution and Commercialized Vice
Sex Offenses (other)
Narcotic Drug Violation
Gambling
Offenses against Family and Children
Driving under the Influence
Liquor Law Violations
Drunkenness
Vagrancy
All Other Types of Offenses

revenge if they should report the assailant. All of these issues are compounded by the fact that, while some police reporting may be somewhat improved, systems vary widely across the country, and there is no way to be sure that the same crimes are being reported with the same accuracy across the country. Even with these limitations, however, the data do reveal clear and dismaying trends that call for our attention.

The Extent of Violence in America

The extent of violence in our country is frightening. Although we may be more violent than other nations in general, the level of violence within the country is not a constant. Some periods are worse than others, and our own era is one of those high-risk periods. In 1993, 24,526 murders were committed in the United States. That represents sixty-five murders a day. In addition, there were 18,000 assaults per day, with 6,000 of these assaults causing physical injuries.

Although these figures seem straightforward, we are frequently presented with conflicting information about crime. The government reports that it is declining somewhat, yet the media report crimes that seem increasingly aggressive. Which is accurate? Since crime levels fluctuate, we need a clear analysis of these major trends in crime to make sense of these conflicting reports and to fully understand what is happening to us at the present time. Toward that end, Table 4 presents a comparison of the major crime levels in 1960 with those in 1992 from national data compiled by statistician Adam Dobrin and his colleagues (1996). These data present several important findings. Unlike our own day, the period of the early 1960s was generally a low-crime period and serves as a helpful reference point for comparison with the current high levels of violent crime.

As can be seen in Table 4, the first important finding from the statistics is a staggering increase in all levels of violent crime, even after including for better reporting and an increase in the population. The murder rate has doubled. Rape and robbery have increased fivefold, and aggravated assault has increased sixfold. Although victims sometimes know their assailants, increasingly these crimes are being committed by strangers. Thus, the recent declines in violence reported by the government do not necessarily make us feel more safe, because of the enormous increase in crime levels since the 1960s.

The second finding to emerge from the data is information about the age and gender of the assailants. Here the findings mask two important and opposite trends. One trend is a modest decline

Table 4. Comparative Crime Rates: 1960 and 1992

Type of Crime	Victims*		Age of Assailant	Gender of Assailant	Predominant Race of Assailant
	1960	1992			
Homicide	5.2	10.2	15-44	Male	Nonwhite
Rape	8.7	42.8	15-29	Male	Nonwhite
Robbery	49.6	263.6	15-29	Male	Nonwhite
Aggravated Assault	72.6	441.8	15-34	Male	Nonwhite

* Rates per 100,000

in the number of crimes committed by white and nonwhite adult criminals over the age of twenty-four. The second trend is more ominous because it reflects sharp increases in crime by youth (ages fifteen to twenty-four).

For example, the number of young murderers has tripled in the last ten years to 26,000 in 1994, and the number of juvenile murderers using guns during the same period has quadrupled. While most of this violent crime was committed by young males, these statistics also reveal an increase in violent crimes by young girls. Although about thirteen percent of all youth crime is committed by girls, from 1983 to 1992 there was a twenty-five percent increase in violent crimes by young girls, a rate of increase twice as high as that for young males during this same period. These statistics also point to an increase in youthful black assailants, which in some cases may be as great as three to five times that of white-youth assailants.

These statistics on increased youth violence are ominous and worthy of consideration because there are currently thirty-nine million young people under age ten who will shortly enter their teen years, and these teenage years are typically the high-crime years for each generation. The government recently reported the first small decline of 2.9 percent in youth violence for 1995. If this continues, it is an encouraging sign. But far too much remains to be done.

A third finding from these statistics is also masked, and it is that the victims of violence in America are increasingly America's young. Juvenile crime tends to occur after school hours, especially around 3:00 P.M., and often the victims are innocent youth. The National Center for Health Statistics reported that in 1993 more preschoolers were killed by guns than were police officers and United States soldiers shot in the line of duty. The Center also reported that the number of all children dying from gunfire increased ninety-four percent from 1983 (2,951 victims) to 1993 (5,751 victims).

The final finding from the data in Table 4 is the financial cost to society. Addressing crime requires about 550,000 police in 19,691 federal, state, and local policing agents as well as private security agencies with one and a half million employees. A recent Justice Department survey estimated that crime costs our national economy $450 billion each year with an additional $40 billion for prisons and corrections costs.

Although crime in the United States has come down due in part to the hard work of police and corrections, violence still remains a serious problem. The most recent national statistics from the FBI (2011) reflect both the reductions in violence and the work that remains to be done. The figures per 100,000 for 2011 are presented here to be compared to the figures in Table 4 for 1960 and 1992: homicides 4.7; rapes 26.8; robberies 113.7; assaults 241.1. Since 1992, crime is down in all of these categories but it is still not as low as in 1960, when crime began to increase substantially.

In reviewing the findings in Table 4, it is clear that we do not feel safe because we are *not* safe, in our communities, our worksites, or our homes.

The Emergence of the Postindustrial State

How are we to make sense of these sharp increments in all types of violent crime? This is a complex question, but a helpful first step may be to examine the culture in which these changes took place to see whether there are ways to understand why these events may have increased. In fact, a profound social change took place in the culture during this time period as the United States moved from the industrial state to the postindustrial state, and we begin our inquiry there.

The Industrial State

For much of recorded human history, the human family were small farmers who worked the land, raised animals, and retained a rural lifestyle. This agricultural society underwent a dramatic change in the 1850s. During this period, which continued to the 1970s, energy was harnessed to machines, factories were built, and urban settings began to increase as laborers left the farms for the factories.

This period is known as the Industrial Revolution, and was greatly influenced by science, our understanding of the laws of nature and technology, and the application of those laws to the problems of everyday life. This revolution began when water was harnessed to run spinning looms. It began in Britain and was transported to our own country to Lowell, Massachusetts. In short order, other sources of energy such as steam, coal, oil, electricity, thermal energy, and nuclear energy were similarly harnessed to various types of machines with sharp increases in the amount and variety of material goods, and the country became a dominant world power based on its economic strength.

Great advances in science led to improvements in medicine, sanitation, public health, nutrition, housing, transportation, and communication. A strong economy led to adequate employment, the adequate distribution of goods and services, and an improved quality of life for large numbers of the human family. It was not a perfect system, and there were lean economic years as well as periods of war, but the industrial period created an age of affluence previously unknown in human history. Then in the 1970s, a second major transformation began, and the industrial period itself was uprooted.

The Postindustrial State

This new transformation has emerged in part from the advent of personal computers. With large numbers of the workforce having access to these machines, the thrust of economic activity in the country shifted from manufactured goods to a knowledge-based society which emphasizes thinking, research, and discovery. Instead of manufacturing products like automobiles and television sets, the new workforce concentrates on biotechnology, microelectronics, and health care.

This information explosion was accompanied by a second major event, the development of a global economy. In the global economy, companies of all nations compete to sell their goods and services and compete with companies' workers from any corner of the earth to produce the best quality products in the most cost-effective method. We have seen the impact of this new world order in our country in the form of downsizing, layoffs, and mergers as companies adjust to this internationally competitive environment.

These shifts to an information-based society in a global competitive marketplace have resulted in a three-tiered stratification of our workforce. The first tier comprises the knowledge workers. These are the men and women who are engaged in scientific research and discovery in the sciences, and who explore the role of computer technology for health care, education, and the like, as well as the government leaders at the level of policy development who think out how to put the emerging information to best use for our society as a whole.

The second tier includes those workers who provide services to the knowledge workers. Some of these services are personal, such as those of auto mechanics, hairdressers, and retail store clerks. Others are more directly related to the research and discovery itself, working in banking, finances, real estate, and insurance as well as transportation, communications, and utilities.

The third tier is known as the permanent underclass and includes all of those workers who do not have the skills to belong to one of the first two groups. Without the necessary schooling or training to compete for entrance into the first two tiers, members of the permanent underclass have little hope for future advancement and an improved quality of life for themselves and for their children.

The postindustrial state, this knowledge-based society, is having important impacts on the way we live. Individuals have become more mobile in pursuit of employment; many families now have two wage-earning parents, which necessitates child-care; entire neighborhoods or communities rise and fall in part dependent on whether they have the resources and workforce needed for the postindustrial state. We are in a period of major social upheaval, and will remain so for the foreseeable future. [These shifts have been examined in detail by Drucker (1994), Gordon (1996), and Thurow (1996).]

Values of the Postindustrial State

The industrial state was guided by at least two moral directives from the 1850s to the 1960s: religion as expressed through the Protestant Work Ethic, and the American cultural tradition as expressed in the Declaration of Independence.

In Calvinistic theology, morally good people were thought to be predestined by God to be saved, and these good persons were known by their good works. This theological system and the needs of the industrial state were conjoined, as individuals worked hard to demonstrate their good works, and the economy grew. The Protestant work ethic lent itself to the values of hard work, honesty, self-denial, methodical self-control, sexual exclusivity, and concern for the welfare of one's family and one's neighbors.

The industrial state also drew on the strengths of the Declaration of Independence, which stated that the laws of nature and nature's God were the country's roots, and that each citizen was created with equal inalienable rights to life, liberty, and the pursuit of happiness. These rights were secured by the consent of the governed.

While many still guide their lives by these principles, a radically different set of values is emerging for today's age. Shaped perhaps by natural abundance, instant communication, and freedom of choice, the newer values include a sense of personal entitlement, a focus on material acquisition, and instant gratification of sensate experience.

The sense of personal entitlement emphasizes the importance of the self and its needs with no corresponding sense of responsibility to others or to society at large. Here individuals put their own needs and interests first. While they may allow that they must respect the rights of others, in practice this guideline is soon forgotten or overlooked. The sense of personal entitlement has no moral force other than itself, no transcendent moral authority, and frequently no respect for contractual obligations. Such a view of the self can easily evolve into greed and narcissism with a common outcome of the self versus society.

The focus on material acquisition emphasizes the accumulation of goods and services in their own right, and as a culture we do accumulate. We fill our houses, then fill the attics, then fill the cellars, and then rent extra storage space. We accumulate so many material goods that it is not uncommon for us to have to "enjoy" several of them at once. For example, we turn on the television as we start the microwave for the frozen dinner and talk on the phone as we peruse a current magazine or newspaper. Whereas in an earlier age, material goods might have been used to enhance human interaction (e.g., the family car that permitted a Sunday gathering of the extended family), the newer technologies tend to isolate people from one another as they listen to their headsets, or sit alone before their computer screens. The end result can be a further isolation of people, one from the other.

The third dominant value is instant gratification of the body and its senses. Self-denial and delay of reward are considered obsolete and have been replaced by an emphasis on doing things immediately, running up extensive credit charges, and getting here or there at a moment's notice. This is coupled with a lifestyle of pleasure that emphasizes unfettered sex, drugs, alcohol, intense music, and highly charged lives in general. While in moderation these pleasures sustain life and add occasional zest, in extremes individuals are reduced to anatomy and physiology, and may experience weariness, fatigue, boredom, and ennui.

Early Outcomes of the Postindustrial State

Although we are still evolving in the postindustrial era, we are able to assess some preliminary measure of its impact on the economy and on society itself.

With regard to the economy, it is clear that we are making important strides for the country. Advances in health and biotechnology and technological advances in transportation, communications, and improved manufacturing processes will improve our quality of life and strengthen our gross domestic product. The United States is an important player on the economic world stage.

A preliminary examination of the impact of the postindustrial state on the social fabric is less encouraging. The emergence of a permanent underclass is a serious social concern. Larger groups of unemployed persons, without the skills to be productive citizens, benefit no one. In addition, recent studies have reported the following additional distressing findings.

(1) *Broken Homes.* There is a sharp increase in the loss of intact homes. Divorce is high; desertion is increasing. Out-of-wedlock teenage pregnancies are escalating. Parents are away due to shifts in the workforce and the need to travel great distances for employment. Some parents are also away from home because they are incarcerated for violent crimes.

(2) *Disrupted Family Life.* Statistics from all quarters continue to document unacceptable levels of drug and alcohol use, credit card debt, adultery, nonpayment of child support, family violence between spouses and against children, inadequate housing for families, increasing poverty, and serious social isolation. Stress and depression often follow.

(3) *Inadequate Parenting.* Some surveys report that some inadequate parenting is a function of parents with a sense of personal entitlement, who have no true interest in their own children. More common are parents attempting to master one or two jobs for needed income, to provide adequate day care, and to find quality time for family life. This is not easily done in an era of declining incomes, and often the result

is latchkey children without adequate supervision, without adequate limit setting, without adequate consistency in punishment when warranted, with few true caring attachments to others, and without the ability to learn empathy for others which comes from such attachments. The end result is often feelings of neglect and of being unloved.

(4) *Inadequate Schooling.* As tax receipts have declined, governments have had less monies for local services, and many types of programs, including schooling, have been cut. This is a particularly vulnerable area, for without the necessary education today's young people will never be adequately prepared for the postindustrial state, and will find themselves by default in the permanent underclass. It should not surprise us that schools without permanent teachers, without books and supplies, without computers, without adequate physical structure and so forth cannot adequately prepare students for the world in which they must work and live.

We have seen earlier in the chapter how these four factors were found in the lives of the criminals and delinquents who were studied. Could it be that these four factors which were found in small groups of violent people in earlier times have become so pervasive that they can account for the sharp increases in crime in the past thirty-five years? Could the postindustrial transformation somehow be linked to these increases in violent crime? If this were so, what might be the mechanisms in culture to explain these potential linkages?

Cultural Factors in Violence

Culture may be defined as the customary beliefs, social forms, and material traits of a people. The culture, through its societal institutions of business, government, families, schools, and religions, teaches its members the social norms about how they are to interact with one another in socially beneficial ways so that they are productive citizens for the general welfare of all. Cooperative behavior, joint planning, self-restraint, patience, and concern for others are taught as a means of insuring group survival. These social norms create caring attachments to others and these attachments are fundamental to good physical and mental health and to an absence of violence. In this way the social norms maintain a sense of community.

Cultures change, however, and, while there are evolutionary theories, conflict and systems theories to explain such changes, the structural-functional theory of Émile Durkheim (trans. 1951) appears the most helpful in understanding the impact of our present postindustrial shift.

Durkheim theorized that, in periods of great social upheaval, social norms lose their regulatory force as the social institutions that are the repository of these beneficial guidelines themselves undergo change. In the absence of these moral guidelines, caring attachments are disrupted and individuals feel adrift and not integrated into their normal social networks. The sense of integrated community becomes lost. Durkheim called this tendency for the social norms to lose their regulatory force *anomie*. He supported his theory by reviewing the social disruptions of various countries at various periods in history, and repeatedly found sharp increases in suicides, mental illness, general distress, and violent crime. The emergence of the postindustrial state is just such a period of major social transformation.

Two criminologists and intellectual disciples of Durkheim, Drs. Steven Messner and Richard Rosenfeld (1994) have advanced anomie theory an additional step beyond Durkheim's general theory of cultural change. In their view, the moral voices that reside in government, the family, schools, and religion have been superseded by business and an attitude that any economic end justifies any means, including violence. While this may be true in some cases, it seems unreasonable to single out business by itself. It is the engine that sustains all of us and that has accomplished much. Since ours is a culture that emphasizes personal entitlement and material gain, it perhaps makes more sense to understand that any of our social institutions may be compromised to some extent by these values of entitlement and material gain.

In any case, how might Durkheim's basic general theory of anomie help us understand the possible links between the emergence of the postindustrial state and the recent surge in crime?

First is the act of transformation itself. The social norms and guidelines of the early 1960s were disrupted and their regulatory force weakened. All of our societal institutions were and are in the process of adapting to the new world order. Caring attachments become disrupted and the sense of community is weakened.

Second is the emergence of the permanent underclass, which divides society into the haves and have-nots. The have-nots need to support themselves and their families. If the traditional opportunities for advancement are blocked, some may be forced to criminal acts to survive. Drug dealing as a business venture is one example. Again, the sense of community is weakened.

Third, the values of the postindustrial state themselves further contribute to the loss of community. Personal entitlement, material acquisition, and immediate sensate gratification do not foster concern for the welfare of others. In the absence of broader social norms from our basic institutions that emphasize responsibilities toward others, the problem of community is further exacerbated.

It appears that the anomic conditions of our basic societal institutions, the emergence of the permanent underclass, and the values inherent in the postindustrial state can help us understand in part the broken homes, disrupted family life, inadequate parenting, and inadequate schooling that are associated with much of the violent crime that we have examined. When the cultural sense of community fails, when caring attachments are disrupted, communication and hope often fail as well, and when communication fails, violence may follow.

* * *

In this chapter, we have examined our national culture of violence. We have reviewed the actual levels of crime, the major social transformation of the postindustrial state that occurred during the same time period, and how the cultural risk theory of anomie may help us understand the links between the two. We have also seen how anomie with its cultural deregulation also exacerbates the biological, sociological, and psychological risk factors that we will examine in subsequent chapters.

As grim and depressing as this may seem, however, our own history holds an important lesson for us. During the 1880s and 1890s, there was a similar upheaval in our country with attendant social disruption and violence. Durkheim would probably attribute this to anomie resulting from the Industrial Revolution, a major social transformation that preceded our own. In any case, average law-abiding citizens of this earlier period decided collectively to set limits on unlawful, unacceptable, violent behavior and to improve their quality of lives. So can we. When our understanding of the risk factors for violence and crime is complete, we can design a range of specific strategies to contain and prevent their occurrence.

(Flannery, R. B. Jr. *Violence in America: Coping with Drugs, Distressed Families, Inadequate Schooling, and Acts of Hate.* Riverdale, NY: American Mental Health Foundation, 2012. Chapter 1.)

TWO

Understanding Human Violence

Night and silence! Who is here?

—William Shakespeare

The door to the jail cell slammed shut. He was charged with vagrancy, disorderly conduct and two charges of assault and battery on a police officer. So be it, he thought to himself. Life was not fair, the world was a jungle, and, as his voices had correctly predicted, no one could be trusted—not even the police.

Richard had grown up in a housing project on the other side of town. Both of his parents drank heavily and physically abused each other and himself. He tried to separate them during their fights, but he was small in stature and easily flung out of the way into nearby walls. He learned early on that the world was malevolent and that he should keep his head down and his guard up.

The voices had begun four years ago, when he was sixteen. These voices were his regular companions and their directives to harm himself or others were harsh and uncompromising. They particularly cajoled him to attack others first before those others came after him. He was frightened by the voices and had begun to use alcohol to calm his nerves.

Today's dark journey had played itself out at high noon. This morning his voices had been especially intense. He had used some alcohol to self-medicate, but with no measurable relief. He had gone to the park in search of solitude. However, his ill-

kempt appearance and his constant pacing frightened nearby children and the police were called. The police surrounded him just as the voices had predicted that they would. This was the jungle made real.

The police told him to stand still. He was unable to stop from pacing. The police asked his name. He remained mute. One of the officers remembered the police academy instructor saying that, when communication fails, violence follows, but what do you do when the suspect will not speak? In the end, four officers rushed him. He lowered his head and fought as hard as he could. One officer sustained a broken wrist; a second, a scraped face.

Thus, the police had placed him in a cell and slammed shut the door. He wondered if they understood that in the jail cell of his schizophrenic illness the terror and loneliness were worse than anything the state had to impose.

When communication fails, violence follows.

Even though there is a good deal of violence in the world, when it erupts close to home in one's neighborhood by neighbors that everyone considered to be normal, people become frightened and confused. Violence teaches each of us how tenuous our links are to Mother Earth and murders, rapes, assaults, and the like remind us how vulnerable each of us truly is.

This chapter focuses on the evil of human-perpetrated violence on others and examines the various theories to explain such behavior. The initial response of many nonvictims is to assume that the violent person was out of his or her mind, as is the case in our chapter vignette. Yet, only a small percentage of human violence can be attributed to mental illness. This is a cold reality with which it is difficult to come to terms. In most instances, the violent acts were committed by violent persons who were not mentally ill and who were aware of what they were doing. Some behaved impulsively (behavior without thought) and, even worse, some behaved with premeditated, calculated hatred. In the latter case, the assailants clearly knew what they were about.

Why do people commit these heinous acts, including harming helpless children? What motivates or drives them to behave this way? The answer is complicated and not yet fully understood in medicine and science. However, behavioral science has developed and researched several theories that explain what may be at work in any given person's violent behavior. Often, more than one factor is at work in the same violent person.

Understanding what motivates a particular assailant is helpful information for those of us who respond to behavioral emergencies. Knowing, for example, that a person is intoxicated, seeking initiation into a local street gang, or suffering from infarct dementia provides us with information on how to differentially approach a particular patient or client to begin to defuse the risk for potential violence, so that safety for everyone is maintained.

There are four groupings of theories of violence: cultural, biological, sociological, and psychological and each is reviewed in due course. However, we will begin with the three basic principles of good physical and mental health because in each act of violence one or more of these domains is disrupted in the assailant. Moreover, each of these three domains also furnishes health-care providers with some basic intervention strategies to employ in defusing the potential for violence that is associated with their disruptions in behavioral emergencies.

The Domains of Good Health

Caring attachments to others, reasonable mastery in our lives, and a meaningful purpose in life are the three domains of human functioning that lead to good physical and mental health. Adequate functioning results in less anxiety and depression, less illness, and a sense of well-being. The absence of adequate functioning in these domains leads to the loss of a sense of well-being, increased illness, and a shortened lifespan. Anger and violence frequently accompany domain disruptions.

Caring Attachments to Others

Caring attachments are the meaningful bonds or links that we have with other humans. Humans are social animals and being close to others makes us feel good. The absence of others in our lives leads to a loneliness that can be very painful.

World War II in part provided the impetus to study the nature of human attachments. The war had disrupted many families through death, abandonment, and relocation. As families were torn apart, many children became orphaned and society did its best to understand how best to help these children. René Spitz (Lynch, 1977) was among the first to call attention to the importance of human contact and demonstrated how literally deadly could be its absence. In 1945–46, he studied ninety-one infants in orphanages in Canada and the United States. All of them were well cared for by staff but thirty-four died during the last three months of their first year of life. They wasted away in spite of good care and no obvious medical disease. Spitz wondered if the absence of the biological parent(s) in some way contributed to their early death.

During these same years, a British physician, J. Bowlby (1982), was also studying the importance of the mother for the growth of the child. It was obvious that a child was dependent on his or her parents for survival and for learning over time how to survive on its own. Bowlby felt that a child was born with a need to interact socially as a way of meeting these survival goals and Dr. Bowlby set about clarifying the nature of this process. Bowlby observed a child was content in the presence of its mother but, if the mother left the child, the child would scream in protest until its scream brought about the return of the mother and with her return the implications for safety. Bowlby called this mother/child bond an *attachment* and termed the child's distressed screaming in her absence a form of *separation anxiety*. He also noted that, in those cases where the mother did not return, the child would become despondent and depressed. The child remained detached from others, as if not wanting to be abandoned again. When the attachment was secure and consistent, the child's growth and development were normal and adaptive. In those cases where the attachment was insecure or absent, the child's growth was not normal and a variety of problems emerged over time.

Subsequent research has studied the nature of adult attachments. Attachments to family, friends and colleagues bring us companionship, emotional support in good times and bad, information about solving life-stressful problems, and instrumental favors in the forms of money or political influence on our behalf (see review in Flannery, 2004a). Other types of attachment, however, may prove to be harmful. These include those marked by physical or sexual abuse, emotional over involvement in others, emotional demanding-ness, interpersonal skill deficiency, and the like.

One additional important component of caring attachments is mastering the skills of empathy. Empathy refers to our ability to understand the feeling states of others. This process is usually begun in childhood when parents teach their offspring how other children and adults feel. For example, a mother might say to her child, Do you remember when grandma died and you felt sad? Well, Jimmy's grandmother has died and he may feel sadness as you did, when your grandma died. This ability to walk in another person's shoes, to understand how they may be feeling forms the basis of empathy and is learned gradually over time. It is a complex skill.

It is also important in understanding some forms of violent behavior. Empathy forms the psychological basis for moral values to take root. Without empathy, it is rare for individuals to have true moral development. In some cases, the violent person harms another because the violent person has limited capacity to appreciate the suffering that he or she is inflicting on the victim.

In addition to the psychological components of caring attachments, physiologist James Lynch (1977; 2000), was studying the physiological components of caring attachments at the same time as the psychological studies were being conducted. He found that a person's cardiovascular system (blood pressure and pulse), the person's immune system to fight upper-respiratory infections, and a person's endorphins endogenous opioid system (chemicals in the brain that make us feel good) were all strengthened in the presence of caring attachments. The reverse was true in socially isolated people. Indeed, he found that the absence of caring attachments resulted in premature death. Clearly, caring attachments are an important domain in good health.

Reasonable Mastery

Reasonable mastery refers to one's ability to shape the environment to meet one's needs. We learn work skills to earn money to eat, we learn social skills to make attachments, and so forth. These types of efforts enable us to pursue our goals in life and to enhance our quality of life, once we have met our basic goals.

Good problem-solvers have a basic set of cognitive strategies that they utilize to solve the issues and problems in life that confront them. First, they correctly identify the problem to be solved. If they are angry at something at work, they do not take that anger out on their family. Second, they gather information about how to solve the problem. They draw on past experience, reading, advice from friends, and the like. Third, they think out carefully specific solutions for the specific problem. They have more than one solution because they know that the world is complex and that their first solution may not work. Fourth, they implement the proposed solution, and, fifth, they evaluate it to see if it actually solved the problem.

Adaptive problem-solvers know something else. They know that they have the mental capabilities and physical strength to solve many problems in life but they also realize that total mastery of everything in life is unreasonable. Some problems they know they do not have the skills to solve. In other cases, they have tried their best but the problem remains unsolved. At some point, they know enough to stop trying and they put their energies to better use.

Poor problem-solving may result for many reasons, including medical or psychiatric illness, disability, inadequate parenting, poor schooling, or being emotionally overwhelmed and unable to think clearly.

Meaningful Purpose in Life

All of us need some reason to get up in the morning and invest our energies in the world around us. This purpose provides the motivation for us to move forward, especially during life's difficult moments. Many years ago, sociologist Aaron Antonovsky (1979) was the first to establish the importance of a sense of a coherent, meaningful purpose in life. One's meaningful purpose needs to provide a sense of the world's manageability, to make the world comprehensible, and to provide a belief that the world is worthy of our investing energy in it. The components of the sense of coherence help us keep life in perspective and buffer the stress of life.

Humans are biological in part, yet have a conscious awareness of their own physical being. We know that our physical self will die at some point, so our conscious self tries to find a way to live on in the minds of others after our deaths. Thus, many successful meanings in life revolve around concern for others. These might include one's children, one's life-work, a community social cause, an artistic creation. This concern for others, in our meaningful purpose in life, is more robust than some of society's other proffered goals, such as money, power, fame, and fortune. These other worldly proffered goals all end in death and do not necessarily leave a legacy that is remembered by others. A meaningful purpose in life that is primarily centered on the self may result in an unnecessarily enhanced sense of self. This exaggerated sense of personal control will some day encounter a problem it cannot solve and at that point its sense of purpose may fail and serious depression may ensue.

Caring attachments, reasonable mastery, and a meaningful sense of purpose in life are the three domains of good health that foster normal moral childhood development and adaptive adult functioning. In the theories of violence to which we now turn, the domains are disrupted or absent and normal moral growth has not developed.

Theories of Human Violence

The theories of violence are many and varied and Table 1 presents a schematic overview of the most common explanations. No one single theory of violence can explain all of the various forms of violence and often there is more than one type of violence present in any given incident, as we have noted earlier. Understanding these various forms of violence may provide health care professionals with an awareness of what to expect and how to approach any given behavioral emergency. We begin with the cultural theories of violence because the presence of cultural roots of violence exacerbate the other three forms of violence. The interested reader will find these theories of violence discussed in much greater detail in Borak (2006), Defelm (2006), and Flannery (2000).

Table 1. Theories of Human Violence

Cultural:	Anomie
Biological:	Genetics Cortex/Limbic System Medical Illnesses
Sociological:	Poverty Inadequate Schooling Discrimination Domestic Violence Substance Use Easily Available Weapons The Media

Psychological:	Mastery
	    Personal Self-care Skills
	    Interpersonal Skills
	    Academic Skills
	Motivation

Cultural Theory

Culture may be defined as the customary beliefs, social forms, and material traits of a people. Although there have been many cultural theories of violence, the theory of Émile Durkheim (1858–1917) has gained the most prominence and many adherents.

Durkheim believed that culture exerted its influence through society's five basic social institutions: government, business, family, school, and religion. He saw these five institutions as the transmitters or educators of a culture's values and social norms. These institutions showed citizens what was expected, what was valued, how to be a productive member of society, and how to interact in socially approved ways with others. The adults then knew in turn the rules by which to raise their children. The end result of this process was an integrated social community in which people had caring attachments, reasonable mastery, and a meaningful sense of purpose. This adaptive regulation of social behavior led to a sense of cohesion in the community and a sense of belonging in the individual.

Durkheim's theory also predicted that, when a society underwent a major social upheaval, society's five basic social institutions would themselves undergo this upheaval, and the commonly agreed-upon set of rules to regulate social behavior among citizens would be in disarray. The sense of social cohesion and belonging would be lost. Durkheim referred to this state of loss as *anomie*. Durkheim supported his theory by reviewing all of the countries that had been through major social upheavals throughout history. He noted that after each upheaval the cohesion and sense of belonging were repeatedly replaced by increases in mental illness, substance use, suicides, and human-perpetrated violence toward others.

Many social scientists (e.g., Drucker, 1994) believe that we are in just such a major social upheaval in our own age. From 1850 until about 1970, our culture was referred to as the Industrial State. The Industrial State was characterized by the harnessing of energy to run machinery. The Industrial State became a society that produced goods and services based on ever expanding technological advances. These years were governed by a value system commonly known as the Protestant Work Ethic. It stressed concern for the welfare of others, especially the young and the elderly; hard work; honesty; self-control; self-denial to improve the lot of one's children; and sexual exclusivity in marriage. Although poverty and various types of discrimination remained, over time an increasing majority of citizens came to have caring attachments, reasonable mastery, and a sense of meaningful purpose that was rooted in concern for others.

The 1970s marked what Durkheim would see as a major social upheaval. Society moved from providing goods and services to creating knowledge after the advent of computers. Whereas an employee in the Industrial State might have physically made motor vehicles, in this new age, known as the *postindustrial state*, that same employee provided services and information by means of the computer. For example, an employee might enter insurance claims on a computer. Moreover, a new value system has emerged to replace the Protestant Work Ethic. Postindustrial values emphasize the self first, material goods, and instant gratification.

As Durkheim foresaw, the five major societal institutions have themselves been caught up in this transition. The common agreement on acceptable social behavior has been lost with a resultant decline in the sense of community cohesion and belongingness. Mental illness, substance use, suicide, and violence toward others have all increased in our age and many of today's citizens do not have caring attachments, reasonable mastery, or a meaningful sense of purpose. It is likely that this transition to the postindustrial state will continue for several more decades before a commonly agreed-upon set of socially integrated values and guidelines emerges. Without a sense of integrated community and belongingness, our cultural backdrop to violence will continue for some time to come.

Biological Theories

Many medical and behavioral scientific researchers have asked a fundamental question: Do abnormalities in biological structure and function result in violence? The answer is a complex and qualified "yes" in some, but not all, cases.

A first reasonable question is to ask whether there is any evidence to suggest that violence is genetic and inherited. The question is asked in part because some families are violent in succeeding generations and in part because some crimes are so heinous that most of us want to believe that there must have been some abnormality in the assailant at birth.

The research evidence to date is mixed. Some researchers such as Bouchard (1994) suggest that there is no known genetic basis for violence. Different violent persons committing the same crimes have no common genetic component. However, other investigators such as Guan Guo and his colleagues (Guo, Roettger, and Cai, 2008) report that the MAOA gene, the dopamine Transporter1 gene, and the dopamine D2 receptor gene in the presence of environmental stress may link adolescent delinquency to molecular genetic variants. Further genetic research is needed before conclusions may be drawn.

There is research evidence that documents that injury to the brain in the cortex or limbic system may result in violence. Tumors, head injuries, viruses, birth defects, and exposure to lead are some of the events that may destroy the cortex and its cortical control centers that inhibit violent behavior. Similar injuries to the limbic system such as viruses, head injuries, and untreated psychological trauma may result in violence as well.

Certain medical and psychiatric illnesses contain the potential for violence. Some examples of medical conditions that may result in violence would include Alzheimer's disease, delirium, glycemic conditions, lupus, multiple sclerosis, Parkinson's disease, seizures, thyroid conditions, and traumatic brain injuries. Some examples of psychiatric conditions that may be associated with violent outbursts include attention deficit/hyperactivity disorder (ADHD), depression, psychological trauma, serious mental illness, substance abuse, and suicide. Not every person with these various illnesses will become violent but some may. In these latter cases, biology may be a contributing factor.

Certain bodily conditions may also elevate the risk for violence. These include states of pain, hunger, sleep deprivation, excessive heat, overcrowding, and/or life stress.

Four personality disorders—antisocial, borderline, narcissist, paranoid—have been at times associated with violence (American Psychiatric Association, 1994). The level of biological involvement in these personality disorders remains medically unclear. However, unlike some medical illnesses, there is no current evidence that these personality disorders and associated violence are necessarily beyond an individual's control. An antisocial person is one who is engaged in criminal activity toward person or property, is not governed by the prosocial values of society and is often morally depraved. The person with borderline disorder has intense mood swings from uncontrollable crying to intense oral hostility and rage. Some researchers believe that persons with borderline personality disorder may have a limbic system dysfunction. A narcissistic person is one who values oneself above all else and continuously wants one's own way. The individual with a paranoid personality is suspicious of most all persons and events. The world is seen as a hostile threat that requires constant vigilance to assure one's safety.

Recent Biological Findings. There have been recent advances in our understanding of the possible biological roots of violence. Understanding how recent advances might explain this violence requires a brief understanding of three components of the brain. First is the cortex. This is found at the top of the brain just under the skull. This is the part of the brain that takes in information from the senses, rationally evaluates what is to be done, then implements those decisions (we hear the growling dog, we decide it is dangerous, we move away). The second component is the old brain stem (OBS). It is at the back of the head and controls needed vital life functions that we do not need to think about, such as beating of the heart, becoming hungry, etc. The limbic system is the third component. It is tucked up under the cortex and OBS and is where feelings first register in the brain. These feelings are then sent to the cortex for rational evaluation within the individual's value system.

Recent research has confirmed that the brain does not fully mature until age 25. Until then, the feelings in the limbic system may exert more sway over the individual than rational thought. For example, an angry teenager may commit an act of vandalism rather than seeking to solve the problem through higher cognitive verbal conflict resolution. This finding is important since many acts of violence are committed by young people where a biologically immature brain may be a contributing factor.

Recent research has also yielded a better understanding of the OBS's links to violence. When an individual is overwhelmed, the rational, thinking cortex may shut down in some cases and the

OBS may become fully activated. In these situations, the individual may go into survival mode. In situations of overwhelming anger and/or anxiety, violent behavior may emerge as a form of self-defense. This "kill or be killed" mindset may be found in some victims of untreated posttraumatic stress disorder (PTSD). (See Chapter 3.)

Lastly, there are chemicals in the brain that carry information from one nerve fiber to the next, from one brain component to the next. These chemicals are called neurotransmitters. When these chemicals are present in the proper amounts, the brain functions normally. If the chemicals are not in the present amounts, the brain does not function properly and abnormal behaviors may occur. Violence is one possible outcome. Serotonin is a neurotransmitter that makes us feel calm and happy. If serotonin is depleted, an individual may feel and act in angry ways and, if serotonin is greatly depleted, an individual may become suicidal. Another neurotransmitter, known as dopamine, searches out pleasurable experiences for the individual. When it finds one, it searches again for the same pleasure. However, if dopamine is overused in this pursuit, it changes body chemistry such that the individual will need several exposures to obtain the same pleasurable state. This may be part of the explanation of why addictions worsen over time. Since much violence is perpetrated by individuals abusing substances, this biological neurotransmitter may need to be considered in some violent acts.

Some acts of violence appear biologically rooted and disrupt the domain of reasonable mastery. However, the total numbers of these cases is small and can in no way account for the total levels of present-day violence in our society.

The biological theories have their main impact on disruptions in the domain of mastery and to some extent meaningful purpose.

Sociological Theories

The sociological theorists of violence seek to explain what social environmental events in our daily lives may contribute to violence. The research has focused on poverty, inadequate schooling, discrimination, domestic violence, substance use, easily available weapons, and the media. Since these issues are routinely discussed in the media and are familiar subjects, they will be noted here briefly.

It has been known since the time of the Romans that poverty is highly correlated with crime and violence. In some cases, individuals without financial resources are forced to steal to feed, clothe, and shelter themselves. Some without adequate prosocial problem-solving skills earn a living by engaging in criminal behaviors, such as fencing stolen goods, fraud, or drug-trafficking. Still others who learn of the emphasis on material goods through the media break and enter, snatch purses, and commit robberies to obtain the material goods that they cannot legitimately afford.

Inadequate schooling compounds the problem of poverty in the postindustrial state. Knowledge and technology continue to become increasingly complex and those who drop out of school or who come from inadequate schools do not learn the socially sanctioned skills and educational skills necessary to obtain employment in the knowledge-based state. Schools without enough teachers, without enough books for each student, without adequate computer availability, and schools in physical disrepair do not adequately prepare children for earning a living in today's age.

Acts of discrimination are acts of hatred committed against innocent persons because of some aspect of their personhood. Age, race, ethnicity, creed, gender preference, and physical attributes are some of the more common areas of discrimination known to all of us. Every act of discrimination blocks some person or persons from equal access to basic civil rights and equal opportunities.

Domestic violence refers to violence committed by any family member or significant other toward any other family member or significant other. Such violence may involve grandparents, parents, children, extended family members and a variety of significant others who may be residing in the home. The abuse may include murder, physical and sexual abuse, nonverbal intimidation, verbal abuse, neglect, and/or mental torture. This is a serious problem encountered by health-care providers and is the subject matter of a later chapter.

Substance use is a serious national public health problem and includes the excessive use of alcohol and a variety of street drugs and prescription medications. Many times the substance use begins as a form of self-medication to soothe one's nerves but over time it becomes a physical addiction. Substance use impairs the individual's physical health and social well-being in terms of family disruptions, loss of employment, legal involvement, and similar. It is important to remember that substance use disinhibits the higher cortical-control centers in the brain and increases the potential for behavioral violence.

The presence of easily available weapons, especially those for purchase by children and adolescents in school playgrounds, has led to the increased use of firearms to settle conflicts over girlfriends, boyfriends, money, loss of face, and the like. Whereas in the past, the two parties might have had a fist fight, now each party is brandishing a weapon. So extensive is the problem, that innocent children now feel that they have to arm themselves for protection, when they leave home. Legitimate gun holders who are licensed and use their weapons appropriately, such as for hunting, should be supported but society needs to address the presence of easily available weapons for children in our school neighborhoods.

Finally, the impact of the media needs to be addressed. There is an extensive national debate currently about whether video games increase the marksmanship of children. For some, it no doubt does but, as with the portrayal of violence in other media forms, most children who watch these violent episodes do not then become copycat assailants. There is a small subset of children who are unduly influenced by the violence in the media, including computer games. Further research is needed to identify these high-risk children. In the interim, society in general would benefit from parents engaging in media literacy with their children. Media literacy refers to educating the child as to the true and full meaning of what is being viewed. For example, after a scene of a violent car accident, the parent might discuss the importance of safe driving, the impact of the accident on the victim's health, the impact of the accident on the victim's family, and so forth. Discussions such as these teach children about the painful consequences of violence that are not portrayed in the media as it cuts to commercials.

In general, the sociological theories reflect disruptions in the domain of caring attachments and often reflect lack of empathy as a component.

Psychological Theories

The psychological theories refer to two main factors: the individual's coping skills and the individual's motivation for violent behavior. Coping skills refer to personal self-care skills, interpersonal skills, and academic skills. Self-care skills include sound health and nutrition practices, the importance of exercise, understanding the financial system, managing time, managing life-stress, and learning how to comfort oneself in personally difficult times. Interpersonal skills refer to an ability to interact well with others and include being able to identify our feeling states correctly, having empathy for others, expressing our needs tactfully, sharing with others, grieving, and using verbal-conflict resolution skills to solve interpersonal problems. Academic skills involve not only computer literacy but a strong foundation in all basic academic areas, including math, science, English, English composition, and history among other subjects.

The absence of these adequate coping skills, coupled with the absence of caring attachments, leaves the person without the prosocial skills and contacts to participate fully in the postindustrial state. In the face of this inability to participate in more socially acceptable ways, many turn to antisocial values. Their behavior is motivated by catharsis, anger, selfishness, self-indulgence, the enforcement of one's personal sense of justice, social acceptance in gangs, shame, and similar self-defeating motivational stances: see Table 2.

The psychological theories result in disruptions in the domains of reasonable mastery and meaningful purpose.

This overview of the theories of human violence may be helpful for those of us in professional care-giving roles, if we link these theories to our discussion of the domains of good health. As we have noted, each grouping of theories implies the disruption of one of these basic domains that results in the increased risk for violence: the cultural theories with the destruction of caring attachments, the biological theories with disruptions in mastery, the sociological theories with disruptions in attachments, and the psychological theories with shattered reasonable mastery and a prosocial meaningful purpose in life. An important message is that, when encountering behavioral emergencies with potential for violence, look for small ways to restore a sense of attachment, a sense of reasonable mastery, and a sense of some meaningful purpose.

Table 2. Common Motivational Factors in Violence

Acceptance by Peers
Catharsis of Anger
Despair
Dominance of Others
Enforcement of Personal Sense of Justice
Excitement
Jealousy
Revenge
Selfishness
Shame
Status

(Flannery, R. B. Jr. *The Violent Person: Professional Risk Management Strategies for Safety and Care.* Riverdale, NY: American Mental Health Foundation, 2009. Chapter 2.)

THREE

Psychological Trauma

*Never shall I forget those moments that murdered my God
And my soul and turned my dreams to dust.*

—Elie Weisel

It was about 8:15 on a Tuesday morning. Evan sat quietly at home in his recliner chair and listened to soft music on the radio. As the words and melody to "Raindrops Keep Falling on My Head" began, he lurched out of his chair as if propelled by a cannon shot. He lay writhing on the floor, his pulse was over 140, his blood pressure was 175/110. His body was shaking, his teeth chattering, and his bones registering the chill of death, as if he had been left for hours in the cold snows of winter. He gasped for breath. He was crying. He was in sheer terror and inconsolable agony. His dark night of the soul had once again returned.

Raindrops. Raindrops? Raindrops on a bright sunny morning in late summer in New York City? How could that be?

But it was true. There were raindrops. Human raindrops. Persons who had elected to jump from eighty to one hundred floors above to their deaths below rather than burn in the Twin Towers inferno that engulfed them all. Many hoped that they would die of a heart attack on the way down. They called home on cell phones to say one last good-bye to loved ones, then to say a small prayer, and then finally to jump into the abyss.

As a first responder nurse, Evan knew that he could not break these falls because the force of their impact would kill him as well. Thus, he had to stand there helplessly. Many of these precious raindrops did not have fatal heart attacks on the way down but were alive and killed instantly on impact. Evan witnessed the final agonizing screams of death, crushed skulls, broken limbs, and spattered pools of blood, brains, and flesh.

Cell phones rang as loved ones called back for just one last moment together. These cold human raindrops of death had become Evan's dark night of the soul.

Evan has a serious medical condition known as *posttraumatic stress disorder* (PTSD). He is not alone. Many persons have this medical condition. It evolves from untreated psychological trauma.

Psychological trauma is an individual's response to a life-threatening situation, over which the individual has no control, no matter how hard the person tries. Natural and man-made disasters; incineration of buildings; rail, aircraft, and motor-vehicle accidents may all cause psychological trauma. In addition, acts of human-perpetrated violence may do so as well. If psychological trauma is not treated, it becomes PTSD. If PTSD is not treated, the victim will carry the scars of this medical condition to the grave.

Psychological trauma and untreated PTSD are common components in behavioral emergencies. These can come about in several ways. First, the emergency itself may be in response to incidents that can traumatize in and of themselves, such as first psychotic episodes or domestic violence. Here the events themselves may have victimized the individuals involved. Second, the present behavioral emergency that in itself is not necessarily traumatic may create psychological trauma in some predisposed individuals. A person of color at home who has been robbed may become traumatized by derogatory comments by a person at work, as the person remembers being mistreated by the robbers. Third, the present behavioral emergency may be a symbolic reminder of other posttraumatic events and the individual who may not be presently injured may still experience the thoughts, feelings and behaviors of the similar, earlier event. For example, some health-care providers responded to a minor car accident where the sole, uninjured, female victim was running around the car proclaiming that her son was dead. There was no body of her son at the scene.

However, the present accident reminded her of a fatal accident some years before that had claimed the life of her son. Finally, we health-care providers may become victims of psychological trauma ourselves, if we have been direct victims ourselves, if we witness and care for others who have been mangled in all sorts of ways, and/or if they recount what has happened to them.

The suffering of the victims of psychological trauma and PTSD is painful for us care-providers to observe and assist with. However, there is second and ominous implication as well. Untreated psychological trauma and PTSD may lead the victim to become violent in his or her own right at a later point in time. We who respond on-site in a specific critical incident may not know that the present victim has a past trauma history and may be functioning with old brain-stem prominence. Therefore, it is important that we recognize trauma when we see it and know how to respond to such victims to enhance safety and keep the behavioral emergency from erupting into violence.

The Nature of Psychological Trauma and Posttraumatic Stress Disorder (PTSD)

Psychological trauma is a person's physical and psychological response to having experienced, witnessed, or been confronted with events that involve actual or threatened death, serious injury, or threat to physical integrity of self or others (American Psychiatric Association, 1994). It must involve intense fear, helplessness, or horror, such that any adult would be frightened. In children this intense fear may manifest itself in disorganized or agitated behavior. As we noted above, natural and man-made disasters, major technological failures that claim lives, combat, and the many forms of human-perpetrated violence are all potentially traumatizing events in that they are life-threatening and we as individuals have no control over these events, no matter how hard we try.

Any of us may become a victim of psychological trauma in one of three ways. The first is by direct act in which we are attacked, threatened, or directly harmed. The second way is by witnessing these traumatic situations impacting on others. We may be direct witnesses to the incident or, as frequently happens to care-givers, witnesses to the incident's impact and its aftermath on the patient victims that we care for. The third way is through vicarious traumatization. This refers to the care-provider, family member, neighbor, or others who develop psychological trauma, by listening to the victim's recounting of the traumatic crisis.

Domains of Good Health

Traumatic events may disrupt any of the three domains of good health and result in impaired functioning in attachments, reasonable mastery, or meaningful purpose.

Attachments. First, caring attachments may be torn apart. This may be due to the actual deaths and separations of loved ones and/or disruptions in community life. In addition, the victim may perceive the world as not safe and other persons as potential assailants. This latter fear is especially common in human-perpetrated violence and victims withdraw from daily life activity to some perceived safe environment.

The loss of caring attachments is further compounded by the behavior of nonvictims. Traumatic incidents again teach how tenuous our links are to Mother Earth. To provide ourselves with the illusion of some control, we blame the victims for their predicaments. Instead of identifying them as being the wrong person in the wrong place, we blame them for being victims of natural disasters or criminal behavior. "If they hadn't been on the beach, they would not have been swept away in the Tsunami." "If she didn't wear shorts, she wouldn't have been raped." "If he hadn't gone across the city common at dusk, he wouldn't have been mugged." Statements such as these are meant to provide nonvictims with the illusion of control. The implication is that the nonvictims would not be as foolish a risk-taker as the victims and, thus, would be saved from harm. The problem, of course, is that it *is* an illusion and contains no guarantee of safety. The tragedy here is that, at the moment when victims most need caring attachments, those potential caring attachments have pulled away in an opposite direction.

Mastery. The loss of reasonable mastery in traumatic events is self-evident. By definition, these are crises beyond the control of the victims. People with reasonable mastery skills are suddenly overwhelmed. They may respond in any number of ways. They may flee in panic, they may freeze in terror, they may develop learned helplessness, they may become super-vigilant about the smallest of details to prevent a recurrence. They may use drugs or alcohol to self-medicate the terror and chaos. None of these strategies is effective in addressing the crisis but such disrupted mastery behavior may last for hours, days, or years. Each of us has a psychological boundary about ourselves that reinforces our sense of control. It is about a foot in distance and people need permission to come closer inside that psychological boundary. Parents, children, close friends may enter but not strangers. When a traumatic event occurs, the victim's sense of boundaries is torn down and the victim feels helpless in the onslaught of forces beyond the victim's control. It is a very frightening feeling.

Meaningful Purpose. When we got up this morning, each of us made some assumptions about the world around us. We assumed that the world was orderly, safe, reasonably predictable, and worthy of our investing energy in it. For victims of violence these assumptions are often shattered by the nature of the traumatic event. The world does not seem orderly, safe, and predictable after the onset of a sudden, violent incident and it certainly does not feel to victims that they want to remain or become a part of it.

Victims physically and psychologically withdraw. When care-providers arrive to assist, the victim's psychological boundaries for safety have been shattered. The victims are often experiencing the raw, brunt force of the crises and they may well be functioning with old brain-stem prominence. In these cases, they may need health care assistance to reestablish cortical control.

Symptoms of Psychological Trauma and PTSD

As with any medical condition, psychological trauma and its untreated counterpart, PTSD, have signs or symptoms that the mind and body are not functioning properly. When a crisis erupts, certain biological chemicals in the victims are activated to protect the victims but they may also result in trauma/PTSD symptoms.

Our nervous system is a series of nerve fibers joined together by small balloon-like vesicles known as *synaptic gaps:* see Figure 1. These gaps contain chemicals that are known as *neurotransmitters.* These neurotransmitters prepare us so that we are best able to cope with the crisis at hand. Common neurotransmitters include adrenalin, which becomes epinephrine in the body and norepinephrine in the brain; and cortisol, serotonin, and the endorphins.

Figure 1. The Synaptic Gap

(with Neurotransmitters)

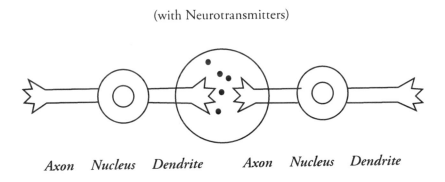

Axon   *Nucleus*   *Dendrite*   *Axon*   *Nucleus*   *Dendrite*

Adrenalin is activated instantly and causes the individual to become immediately attentive. As epinephrine in the body, adrenalin enervates the heart, lungs, and muscles to work effectively and efficiently. Epinephrine dilates pupils, so that potential victims see more clearly and it dampens down bodily functions that are not necessary for immediate survival, such as digestion. Cortisol is released and this provides the individual with increased sources of energy and blood clotting ability to survive wounds.

In the brain, adrenalin becomes norepinephrine and rivets the person's attention to the crisis at hand.

Two additional chemicals are at work in the brain during a crisis. Serotonin, a chemical that normally makes us feel good, is utilized as a catalyst in a crisis to make norepinephrine function more efficiently. Chemicals called endorphins which also normally make us feel good, act as analgesics to deaden pain in a crisis. Various combinations of these neurotransmitters result in the trauma symptoms noted in Table 1.

Table 1. Symptoms of Psychological Trauma and Posttraumatic Stress Disorder

Physical Symptoms	Hypervigilance
	Exaggerated Startle Response
	Difficulty Sleeping
	Difficulty with Concentration, Memory
	Mood Irritability — Especially Anger and Depression
Intrusive Symptoms	Recurring, Distressing Recollections (Thoughts, Memories, Dreams, Nightmares, Flashbacks)
	Physical or Psychological Distress at an Event that Symbolizes the Trauma
	Grief or Survivor Guilt
Avoidant Symptoms	Avoiding Specific Thoughts, Feelings, Activities or Situations
	Diminished Interest in Significant Activities
	Restricted Range of Emotions (Numbness)

The physical symptoms are primarily the result of adrenalin and cortisol in the body. Hypervigilance, exaggerated startle response, difficulty sleeping and concentrating, and angry outbursts reflect the full flow of adrenalin in the victim. It is nature's way of providing the victim every opportunity for survival.

The intrusive symptoms are primarily memories of the event and are thought to be present because of adrenalin and the endorphins being in the brain. The victim keeps reviewing the tragedy day and night in dreams, recollections, nightmares, and the like. Similarly, symbolic reminders of the situation can result in revisiting traumatic events in memory. For example, the ex-combat soldier at home who hears a bus backfire and is reminded of the sounds of artillery shells in war. Finally, grief and survivor-guilt are included as intrusive memories because the grieving survivor is always thinking of those who died in the traumatic event. Intrusive memories appear to be the brain's method of healing itself. It is saying to the victim: review what has happened so that you will be better prepared next time, should it ever happen again. However, these memories are very painful and many victims try to put them out of their minds through various methods of distraction.

The avoidant symptoms are fundamentally symptoms of withdrawal from life. Adrenalin and serotonin appear to have been depleted or used up, a state that leaves the victim weary and depressed. The intrusive memories of the event are a further burden. In these circumstances many victims immediately withdraw from the scene of the traumatic incident and over time withdraw from a whole range of activities in life that were previously of interest. Emotions become restricted. The person is never really happy, never really excited about life, but instead develops a chronic sense of mild to moderate depression. If the trauma/PTSD is not treated, these sufferings will last until death.

Stages of Psychological Trauma and PTSD

Figure 2 outlines the stages or phases that victims of psychological trauma and PTSD may go through. The traumatic event

---

Figure 2. Stages in Psychological Trauma and Posttraumatic Stress Disorder

The Traumatic Event
↓
Acute Distress
↓
Posttraumatic Stress Disorder
↓
Acute PTSD
↓
Chronic PTSD
↓
Delayed Onset PTSD

occurs and acute psychological distress follows immediately. The distress is manifested by disruptions in the three domains of good health and/or by the presence of any of the trauma symptoms. Victims average about thirty days to recover and restore some semblance of normal daily living. This timeframe is based on the amount of time the average victim needs to recover. Traumatic events differ in their severity and people differ widely in their coping skills, so there are understandable individual differences with this time span.

If the victim is still experiencing disruptions in the health domains and/or the presence of symptoms on the thirty-first day, the person develops the medical condition known as posttraumatic stress disorder (PTSD). There are three types of PTSD. The first is acute PTSD, which is defined as disruptions in the domains of good health and/or the presence of trauma symptoms that occurred during the acute distress period and continue for as long as the next three months. If the symptoms continue four months or beyond after the acute distress phase, the victim has developed chronic PTSD with domain disruptions and/or trauma symptoms that will last until death in the absence of treatment. In these chronic PTSD cases, it is not uncommon for a subsequent acute traumatic stress situation to serve as symbolic stimulus or reminder for the recall of memories originally associated with the first traumatic incident.

The last form of PTSD is known as delayed onset PTSD. In these cases, a victim was originally distressed by the event during the acute distress phase but seemed to quickly return to normal daily living. At some point after six months of normal daily routines, the health domain disruptions and/or trauma symptomatology originally associated with the event return in full, vivid, frightening recall. This latent recall is precipitated by a symbolic reminder or by a major loss. All traumatic incidents involve loss such as the loss of physical integrity in battering, the loss of free choice in rape, or the loss of innocence in the world in combat. In this way, loss through death, failing senses, financial reversal, and similar events may result in the return of intrusive memories.

Special Issues in Psychological Trauma and PTSD

There are certain behavioral issues that are frequently found in trauma and that may complicate the victims' lives and recoveries. These include self-medication, dissociation, the repetition compulsion, unresolved grief, and, regrettably, subsequent victim-perpetrated violence.

Self-medication

If one were to go onto hospital wards where victims of psychological trauma were being treated, the patients' charts would likely contain two diagnoses. The first, not surprisingly, would be untreated PTSD. The second diagnosis, however, would be substance use disorder. This would be true in a great many cases. The medical charts of cardiac or cancer patients would not carry frequent diagnoses of co-occurring substance use disorders.

When individuals are victims of violence, they are terrified. They experience disruptions in the domains of good health and the symptoms of trauma and PTSD, as we have seen. Most commonly, they do not realize that they are victims of psychologi-

Table 2. Substance Use and the Self-medication Hypothesis

Substance	Type of Psychological Distress
Amphetamines Cocaine	Depression
Alcohol Barbiturates	Anxiety
Opiates	Anger

cal trauma and they do not realize that they have a diagnosable medical condition for which there is treatment. In their lack of understanding, they turn to drugs or alcohol to calm their nerves and reduce their intense emotional distress.

Psychiatrist Edward Khantzian (1997) noticed that people who abused substances had a drug of choice, if they had the money to buy it. He also noticed that certain favorite drugs of choice were being used to medicate certain types of feelings. Table 2 presents a brief summary of his findings.

Persons using amphetamines and crack/cocaine were self-medicating depression. Persons using alcohol or barbiturates were medicating anxiety, and persons using the various types of opiates (e.g., oxycontin) were self-medicating states of anger and rage. A good many of the self-medicating patients that he observed had trauma histories, so one could speculate that in some cases the feeling states that they were self-medicating, were feelings that came about as a result of their traumatic incidents.

This self-medication information may be of assistance if asked to respond to an emergency in which substance use or a history of substance use are present. Knowing the drug of choice will tell you something about the psychology of your victim and what mood states you might expect, especially if withdrawal is in progress.

Dissociation

When a person is confronted with a life-or-death situation, the person's brain has the remarkable capacity to put out of immediate mental presence all information that is not necessary for survival which, if considered, might distract the person and result in death. If three comrades are in a foxhole in combat and take a direct hit so that only one survives, the survivor's brain will put all unnecessary information aside so that that soldier can focus on survival. The brain will not become preoccupied with the deaths of comrades and increase the risk of the soldier's own death.

This process is known as dissociation and the information that is not needed for survival is temporarily put aside in the person's memory. This is called a dissociated memory. When the crisis has past, this dissociated memory returns to the person's consciousness and is known as a *flashback*. Although these memories are very vivid, they seem to follow the rules of normal memory (McNally, 2003). The victim's review of the dissociated material appears to be the brain's way of reviewing the material to see if anything can be learned in case such a crisis should ever happen again. Since these memories are unpleasant, many victims find some way to distract themselves from these unpleasant thoughts, as we have noted, and in doing so lay the groundwork for the trauma to remain untreated. Victims of combat and rape are the victims most likely to experience dissociative episodes. Flashbacks are most likely to be tripped off by symbolic reminders or by losses.

The Repetition Compulsion

One of the continuing mysteries of psychological trauma is a phenomenon known as the repetition compulsion. One would think that, if you were a victim of violence, that you would move as far away as possible to safety and most victims do. Yet, there is a small group of victims who go back into harm's way, when there is no reason to do so.

I have seen this frequently in health care. Some health-care providers are always in the middle of patient assaults. At first, one reviews the safety procedures of nonviolent self-defense approaches to be sure that staff members are technically skilled. When one is assured of this competence, then one must look for some other explanation for this phenomenon. Certain theorists believe the repetition compulsion is an attempt to learn better mastery skills for better protection in the future (e.g., the sexual-abuse victim who engages in prostitution). Other scientists are studying various possible biological explanations for this phenomenon.

Unresolved Grief

As we have noted, all trauma involves loss of some form. Your family abuses you or walks out on you. Your innocent children are murdered in drive-by gang shootings. Your experiences of incest or sexual abuse leave you feeling like damaged goods. The sexual abuse among ministers challenges your religious faith. If nothing else, human-perpetrated violence shatters your innocence of the world. Since many victims are ashamed of what has befallen them and society's nonvictims do not want to hear about such things, the victim's grief often remains unspoken, unshared, and unresolved.

Although there are several models for understanding grieving, perhaps the most common one is the five-step model of Elisabeth Kübler-Ross (1997). Dr. Kübler-Ross did her studies on patients who were dying, but it turns out that steps for grieving death are similar for any loss (e.g., divorce, not being promoted, financial loss). In Dr. Kübler-Ross's model the first step is denial in which the person refuses to accept the facts of what has happened. For example, a patient might protest that the laboratory tests suggesting cancer are really someone else's laboratory reports. The second step is one of anger. The person facing the loss becomes very angry about the loss and the person's anger can be displaced or placed on others who are innocent bystanders to the loss. In the third step, the person bargains with God, with the doctors, with the powers to be in any individual case to mitigate the loss somehow. The person bargains to have it be less severe or to be put off for some time. In step four the person becomes really depressed as the weight of the loss begins to sink in. Finally, in time, in step five the person becomes resigned to one's fate. Not all people go through all five steps or go through them in the most common sequence outlined here but grieving is an important part of life and must be addressed.

If a person is not fully grieving a loss that is severe or that is protracted over time, that person may develop clinical depression and the need for antidepressant medications. If left untreated, the person may become suicidal. Recent medical research suggests that, at least in some cases, suicide may be a biologically based medical condition. Every year in this country, suicides are about one percent of the population and this has basically not wavered since the Civil War, when medical statistics in our country started to be recorded. In addition, recent research on persons who had completed suicide in Scandinavia showed the brains of these persons to have serious serotonin depletion. This suggests a possible biological basis for suicide in that these individuals were born with less serotonin than normal or that somehow it was used up more quickly than normal and additional research is now being undertaken (Mann, 2003).

Behavioral emergencies by definition imply some sort of loss in health and functioning and caregivers will do well to pay attention to the presence of unresolved grief. One would want to be especially aware of a patient or family member in the second step, that of anger, since that anger in the person's grief may be misdirected in violent ways toward the team that is there to help.

Violence by Victims

An important reason for identifying and treating trauma in behavioral emergency victims is that these early interventions may mitigate and prevent the use of violence at a later time by the patient who is currently the trauma victim being treated. In many cases, victims of untreated trauma and PSTD go on to become violent. Children sexually abused as children have gone on to rape. Children who have been battered as children have grown up to batter others. There are many types of examples of this phenomenon.

Why would they do this, especially when they know how painful it is to be the victim? There are several possible paths toward this end. One, which we just examined, is the anger and depression over what has happened. If the victim's grief for each incident is unresolved, then that anger may surface and others may be victimized. Some victims have learned that violence works, so they use violence as a mode of solving problems. Others want revenge to settle old scores. For still others, the use of substances may have disinhibited the cortical control centers in the brain leading to violence. Finally, as we shall see in the section below, the experience of psychological trauma may change the biology of the brain of the trauma victim, so that the victim is hard-wired to see the world as malevolent and to act accordingly on that perception.

Psychological Trauma and Changes in the Brain

Mentioned in passing earlier in the chapter is the role of neurotransmitters in the development of the symptoms of psychological trauma and PSTD. This section considers two additional changes that are possible in brain functioning in traumatic stress. One is in the prefrontal cortex called Broca's Area and the other is in the limbic system. Both have serious implications for the work of health-care providers.

Broca's Area is found in the left side of the prefrontal cortex and permits the person to tell others what is happening and what they are feeling. Under very severe stress, when old brain-stem functioning is prominent, a person's Broca's Area may temporarily shut down. The person becomes mute and is unable to communicate orally. The person is immobilized and in a state of psychological shock. This state may last as long as several hours and subsides when the immediate overwhelming life-stress has passed.

Figure 3. The Limbic System

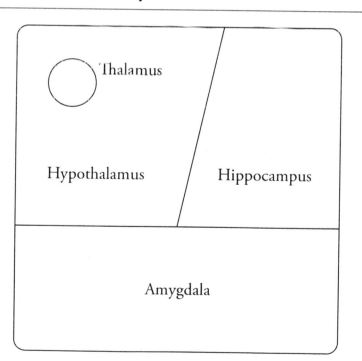

Our second area of inquiry is the limbic system. Figure 3 presents a drawing of the limbic system that is neither anatomically precise nor drawn to scale. In the diagram, the amygdale is that part of the limbic system where emotions are registered in the brain. Feelings of anger, sadness, contentment, excitement and so forth all register here on their way to the cortex. The hippocampus is the part of the limbic system that allows the person to label what he or she is feeling. The thalamus is a relay station for some of the body's sense pathways and sends these sense messages to the cortex. The hypothalamus is the highest center of integration for many visceral processes and, for our purposes here, is the engine that makes the limbic system work smoothly.

Recent research has found that in adult untreated PTSD victims, the hippocampus has atrophied, that is, its cells have died. Without hippocampal language the victim is unable to tell us how he or she is feeling. (In a Broca's Area shutdown, victims would be completely mute.) Hippocampal victims, however, can describe the events, the sequence, and so forth, but they are unable to label their psychological distress. There is some recent research suggesting that an atrophied hippocampus may regenerate itself but further study is needed.

In addition, early and prolonged stress in children results in increased adrenalin for hypervigilance, increased cortisol for the energy to be able to defend oneself, an increase in vasopressin that results in hostility and irritability, a decrease in serotonin resulting in less behavioral control, and a decrease in oxytocin that results in fewer caring, faithful relationships. Many of these changes occur in the limbic system (Teicher, Andersen, Polcari, Anderson, and Navalta, 2002). Additional research on the impact of trauma on the brains of children has shown brain volume to be smaller with fewer language skills and lowered serotonin, which may result in depression and impulsive aggression (Creeden, 2005; Finklehor and Jones, 2006). These early research findings demonstrate clearly that psychological trauma is not good for one's health and normal functioning.

These findings also suggest that severe traumatic stress modifies the brain to live in what it perceives as a malevolent world. The

changes in brain neurochemistry result in suspiciousness, para-
noia, and hypervigilance that lead to social isolation, depression,
and lifelong medical problems such as diabetes and cardiovascular
disease. The brain becomes modified for survival in the jungle and
it is important for all to remember that they may be perceived as
part of the jungle, when they first arrive on-site to provide care.
(For further study of psychological trauma and PTSD, see Flannery [2004] and Herman [1992].)

(Flannery, R. B. Jr. *The Violent Person: Professional Risk
Management Strategies for Safety and Care.* Riverdale, NY:
American Mental Health Foundation, 2009. Chapter 3.)

PART TWO

Risk Management Strategies to Reduce the Risk of Violence

FOUR

Restoring Community:
The Five Social Institutions

*It is the manners and spirit of a people
which preserve a republic in vigor.*
—THOMAS JEFFERSON

*Determine that the things can and
shall be done and then we shall find a way.*
—ABRAHAM LINCOLN

Dateline: Fort Lauderdale, Florida. February 9, 1996.
*The early morning sky was still and full of stars. A southeast
breeze gently pushed the ocean to the water's edge. The air temperature was in the mid-sixties and the water temperature was
seventy-one degrees. Shortly, the first deep purple bands of sunrise would puncture the darkness of the night. It was a special
moment to be alive.*

*In a nearby temporary trailer, the city's beach cleaning crew
was gathering. Known as the Hurricane Crew because of their
ability to clear the city's beaches quickly after natural disasters,
the several men and one woman, a transfer from the cemetery
caretaking division, talked casually as good friends do as they
waited for their next assignment. What they did not know was
that this would be their last assignment. For most, today would
be the day of their death.*

"Love to All" reflected the greeting in the window, but inside anger was the coin of the realm for the homeowner and father of three who was an ex-Marine and decorated rifle expert. For eighteen years he had been a member of the Hurricane Crew, but fourteen months ago, he was fired for drug use and for harassing tourists on the beach.

Things had gone downhill from there. New work had been hard to come by. His wife needed surgery and she became unable to work. When his home hot water failed, he had to send his family away temporarily. He was fired from his security guard position last week, and yesterday he had been rebuffed in his efforts to regain his city position at the beach. Home alone, he seethed in anger.

Fourteen months to the day he lost his city post and less then twenty-four hours after he was rebuffed by the city a second time, the ex-Marine decided to return to work one last time. On this still Friday morning at about five o'clock, he stormed the city's beachside trailer. Armed with two handguns and trained thoroughly by the United States Marines, he methodically murdered five of his former colleagues as they frantically sought to escape. Then, he turned the gun on himself.

The City of Fort Lauderdale awoke. Six of its residents were now widows, and several of its children now had only one parent.

Unemployment. Drugs. Rage. Guns. Death. Another American Dream had ended in pools of blood.

The sunrise came in darkness.

Here is a painful example of violence in the workplace. Homicide is the leading cause of death for women at work and the third leading cause of death for men at work (Flannery, 1995). If we were to ask for suggestions about how to effectively address these homicides at work and the other types of violent crime that we have studied, many of us would suggest more police officers, longer prison terms, the interdiction of illegal drugs, and the like. Intuitively we would mention effective ways to address the biological, sociological, and psychological risk factors. While these suggestions would be correct and helpful in part, in the longer term these approaches would not prove to be fully adequate.

If these three sets of risk factors are exacerbated by cultural anomie, then we need to address that matter as well. If periods of great social change alter the rules for how we are to behave and result in the weakening of community and caring attachments such that violence may result, then our approaches for reducing and containing violent crime will need to include programs that both strengthen community in general as well as addressing specific risk factors in particular. Initiatives that emphasize shared social values, active exchange of ideas, and the search for solutions draw citizens together, foster caring attachments, and strengthen community. Such solutions mitigate the sense of isolation, minimize the negative effects of anomie, and reduce crime and violence.

In the remaining chapters, we will examine approaches to contain and reduce violence in each of our basic societal institutions. We want to examine the many ways in which we can empower ourselves as individuals and as communities to cope with the violent crime around us. Some programs will be familiar and will serve to remind us of the basics that create caring attachments and lessen the probability of violence. Others will be new and will demonstrate the power of human ingenuity in finding solutions to a continuing problem.

In selecting these examples, we will focus on the sociological risk factors. The biological risk factors are reasonably constant as we have seen and many can be successfully treated by medicines. The psychological risk factors for revenge and the like often follow from the perception of sociological injustices, so our attention will be directed primarily toward the sociological factors.

In reviewing what thoughtful citizens have been able to accomplish, we depart from the more formal scientific findings. The solutions that are presented here are best thought of as pilot studies to be further tested by other citizens in other parts of the country, so that we can replicate and learn what strategies are the most effective. Thoughtful solutions will emerge through trial and error.

This overview of effective approaches can also serve as a stimulus to our own sense of creativity. What are our personal strengths? What are our areas of community interest? Where can our efforts make a difference in strengthening the sense of community? Perhaps in individual cases, some will emphasize better parenting, more active school involvement, or a particular neighborhood project. Our solutions will need to be effective and consistent with what we can afford, but our creativity in this search should remain unfettered.

The guidelines and examples presented in these next two chapters are by no means exhaustive. Additional resources and help may be found in Appendix B, the select list by topics of national associations involved in reducing violence. These selected societies cover many issues and are valuable resources for reading materials, for information on proven strategies, and as important networks for linking individuals drawn to common problems. Those individuals interested in starting community initiatives will want to learn what legal or liability issues may be involved. Consulting with the appropriate national associations, as well as with federal, state, or local government agencies, may prove helpful in this regard.

Business

Business can make important contributions toward coping with violence in at least three important ways. The first is to be a well-run, growing, profitable company. Profitability immediately strengthens individuals, families, and communities through payroll expenditures and taxes, and profitability in the longer term permits companies to be socially responsive to basic community needs. Secondly, business can also be of assistance in developing company policies and programs that are family friendly for their employees and that assist employees in finding needed balance in today's age between work and family. Finally, some companies become involved in supporting specific programs that address specific risk factors associated with violence. Each of these three approaches fosters caring attachments, strengthens community, and lessens anomie.

In considering these business approaches, it may be helpful to consider how we might become active in these types of interventions as chief executive officers (CEOs), as managers, as employees, as customers who support helpful companies, and as neighbors who may want to request financial support for a charitable project.

Strengthening Community: Basic Approaches

The Role of Profitability. A profitable business is an asset that strengthens the community where it is located. By employing local residents, purchasing supplies from local merchants, and supporting city services through tax levies, business strengthens the attachments in neighborhoods and communities. Such approaches not only maintain an adequate quality of life, but also contain violence by precluding possible increases in membership in the permanent underclass, at least with respect to its own employees.

This mainstay of the community continues to function quietly each day. Its important role in containing violence is rarely thought of until the business falls upon hard times or closes. All of us know of cities and towns across the country that have been devastated when local businesses have closed or moved away. More often than not, these abandoned communities then face economic downturns, increases in social welfare costs, and, in some cases, increases in violent crime.

Occasionally, this quiet, daily process of community support is highlighted by some major tragedy that demonstrates its importance. Consider the following.

> *Dateline: Lowell, Massachusetts. December 11, 1995.*
> *They gathered in a Boston restaurant to honor a decent and God-fearing man on his seventieth birthday. It was a fitting tribute to the compassion and goodness of the chief executive officer of a fabric company.*
>
> *His company produced eighty percent of the fleece fabric for outdoor clothing, a fabric manufactured from recycled materials, and the business was highly profitable. Thus, it seemed fitting to honor the owner in the twilight of a long and distinguished career.*
>
> *The call came at midnight. There had been a terrible fire. Over thirty employees had been injured. Some seriously. For sixteen hours in forty-five-mile-per-hour winds in the dead of winter, the fire storm raged. It was feared that all was lost.*
>
> *Arriving at his factory, the owner steeled himself. No tears would be permitted.*

He drew strength from his Jewish faith, particularly from Micah 6:8: "He has told you, O Man, what is good and what God really wants from you: Only that you act justly, with loving kindness, and walk humbly with thy God."

But where to begin?

Gathering his several thousand employees, he announced that all of them would be salaried for the next thirty days and have health benefits for the next ninety days. His customers agreed to wait until the plant was up and running again. Donations from companies and individual citizens helped in this effort and within one month eighty-nine percent of the factory was up and running in the buildings that had been spared. Grateful employees worked hard to restore the company. Error rates fell to less than two percent, and a year later there were plans to build a new two-story, 600,000-square-foot textile factory. There was no appreciable loss of market share.

This remarkable CEO who could have easily taken the fire insurance money to finance a leisurely retirement, refused to turn his back on his customers, his employees, his stockholders, and the town that would have been overwhelmed by the permanent loss of his mills.

This fire and its aftermath were important events in the community of Lowell. Buffeted by a recent national economic recession, the city had its share of increased social problems, including violent crime. The loss of the mills would have increased unemployment and further diminished the city's revenue base and might well have jeopardized the city's hard-fought attempts at recovery. Instead of possible chaos, the city and its mills continue to grow two years later, after that fateful winter's day.

The importance of business for the community of Lowell has its counterparts in cities and towns throughout the nation. Profitability strengthens community and decreases the possibility of violence.

As noted earlier, profitability also provides companies with the resources to be socially responsive to other community needs. Here are some examples.

Several companies have chosen health care as an area of corporate concern. Nationally, Service Merchandise raises money for muscular dystrophy; Enesco, a giftware industry, supports Easter Seals; and the RE/MAX real estate employees secure funds for the Children's Miracle Network, a program for hospitalized children. On a more local level, the Ravenna Bank in Ohio supports cerebral palsy victims.

Other companies have focused on the environment. Body Shop International in England produces a range of personal care products that emphasize traditional and native methods of cleansing and softening the skin and hair, as well as environmental issues like minimal packaging and recycling efforts. Stoneyfield Farms, a yogurt manufacturer in New Hampshire, helped preserve several small farms by assisting them in growing organically healthy food products. Similarly, the Wisconsin Electric Power Company, based in Milwaukee, has been involved in several Nature Conservancy Projects statewide. Still other companies such as Coca-Cola and MCI have channeled considerable sums of money for a variety of educational endeavors.

All of these corporate initiatives in their own way contribute to strengthened neighborhoods and greatly reduced crime.

Family Friendly Programs. The emergence of the postindustrial state has changed the nature of the work force, which is now composed of increasing numbers of two-wage-earner couples and single working parents. These parents are hard pressed to meet responsibilities to both work and family, and business has become increasingly responsive to this need with a number of creative solutions that strengthen families at no loss to productivity. Businesses institute these programs for sound bottom-line reasons: increased productivity, less turnover, less absenteeism, and improved employee loyalty and morale. An important, but again often overlooked, benefit from these programs is their powerful effect on containing possible violent crime in families and communities. Each of these family friendly programs fosters caring attachments among family and neighbors, and, as we have seen, caring attachments and meaningful human contact preclude violence.

Family friendly programs are many and varied, but can be divided into two general groupings: work hour arrangements so that parents have more time to be with children, and direct programs that support needed family services.

In the first group, companies have several different approaches. Included are flex-time hours, job sharing, part-time positions, working at home, or compressed work weeks (e.g., working four ten-hour days). Each of these initiatives allows the parent(s) to shape his or her work week and family responsibilities so that both sets of responsibilities are met with less life stress.

Supporting these work hour choices are an additional array of company benefits to support employee dependents: childbirth leave, paid maternity leave, a phase-back period to the worksite for new mothers, adoption aid, sick days that can be utilized when children are ill, dependent care monies for children and elder-services are some of the more common initiatives.

Eli Lilly, Hewlett Packard, IBM, Johnson and Johnson, and Xerox Corporation have been consistent leaders in the area of family friendly programs and their numbers are increasing. *Business Week* and *Working Mother* magazines publish surveys of family friendly companies.

Strengthening Community: Special Areas

The third approach by business to addressing the problems of violence in communities is to support specific programs that are designed to ameliorate the negative impact of specific sociological risk factors. Many businesses are again quietly engaged in such programs as part of their corporate mission. Here is a representative sample of some of these initiatives that address differing risk factors.

The Permanent Underclass. Several companies have created programs that directly address issues of poverty. Northwest Airlines, Target department stores, and Honeywell Manufacturing support Habitat for Humanity International. The Habitat program, begun over twenty years ago, has provided housing for over fifty thousand people worldwide. The Adidas footwear industry has become a citywide corporate sponsor of junior varsity league teams in the boroughs of New York City on the assumption that sports keep students in school. The Honda automobile company has created the Eagle Rock program in Colorado, which teaches individuals basic skills for life and work, and The Body Shop has started projects in New York City to employ the homeless and youth-at-risk in Baltimore, Maryland.

Domestic Battering. The Polaroid Corporation has been exemplary in these matters. Not only have they supported their own employee victims of domestic violence, but they have worked with community agencies to address this need at the neighborhood level. In Quincy, Massachusetts, the company worked with police, corrections, the courts, social service agencies, and shelters for battered women to create a model integrated program to address this need. In a state where domestic violence results on average in one death every ten days, there has not been one death from spousal abuse in this city since the day that the program was fielded. Similarly, the Healthtex Corporation, a leading manufacturer of children's wear, has donated some of its children's garments to a shelter for battered women and children.

The Media. A number of corporations address the issue of violence in the media by presenting programs in the arts totally unrelated to violence. The Aventa Corporation, a financial company, sponsored a museum exhibit at the Philadelphia Museum of Art. Thompson/RCA, an electronics firm, sponsors performing arts programs for high schools in Indianapolis. The Group W/Westinghouse Broadcasting Corporation sponsored a year-long series of media programs on alternatives to violence, whereas the Blue Fish Clothing Company of New Jersey has sponsored a series of hands-on art workshops for inner-city schools in Philadelphia.

In each of these examples, companies have directly addressed sociological risk factors to strengthen community in ways that normal business activity might not. There is still one more area where business can provide important leadership to reduce the risk of harm to customers and employees—the area of violence in the workplace.

Violence in the Workplace

There are several effective strategies to contain or minimize the risk of such violence, and some of the more common ones are presented in Table 1.

Table 1. Addressing Violence in the Workplace: A Checklist

Securing the Facility
   Controlled Access
   Ongoing Surveillance

Warning Signs of Potential Loss of Control
   Appearance
   Behavior

System of Self-defense

Corporate Policy
   Pre-employment Screening
   Employee Assistance Program
   Threat Team
   Buddy System

Securing the Facility. The first risk-management strategy is to secure the physical plant of the facility from easy access to criminals. This is accomplished through controlling access and through ongoing surveillance.

Controlled access is preventing crime by environmental changes that enhance the probability of the assailant's being caught. Since most criminals depend on the element of surprise, when that is removed, criminals are likely to move on to other targets. Controlled access permits only those with legitimate reasons to be in the building to gain entry.

Keeping shrubs around the building low and at a distance from the building, having adequate lighting, keeping windows clear for visibility both inside and outside, and having an adequate number of employees on-site are all associated with less crime and violence.

Access is further controlled by the use of appropriate locks, bolts, electronic admissions systems, cameras, mirrors, and displayed television monitors. All of these suggest to the criminal that the chances of being recognized and apprehended outweigh the risks of the possible criminal behavior.

Ongoing surveillance is the second step in securing the facility. Once legitimate employees and customers have gained access, the company wants to be sure that intruders do not enter during the course of business hours. The cameras, mirrors, and electronics that we have discussed above are also helpful in ongoing surveillance. To these should be added some system of photo identification for regular employees and special passes for visitors. All visitors to the facility should readily stand out. It is also helpful to develop an emergency notification system with call buttons under desks or some sort of coded message for use in any public address system within the building.

Early Warning Signs. All employees and managers will want to learn the early warning signs of impending loss of control and practice how to summon assistance immediately. Early warning signs may be noticed both in appearance and behavior: a general state of dishevelment or disorganization, tense facial expressions, glazed eyes (usually due to substance abuse), and the wearing of sunglasses indoors (possible signs of paranoid thinking or substance abuse) serve as potential warning signs to observers.

Similarly, behavioral signs of severe agitation such as pacing, pounding, stammering; verbal threats toward specific persons; threats of weapons; and obvious signs of substance abuse, such as alcohol on the person's breath should again alert employees to the possibility of tenuous control and impending aggression. The presence of these signs does not necessarily mean that violence will follow, but these signs do bear watching. In general, the greater the number of signs present at any one time, the greater the likelihood of loss of control. Employees should be alert to the possible need to summon help.

System of Self-defense. Companies whose employees deal directly with the public in frequent cash transactions are especially at risk for violence. Taxi cab companies, liquor stores, gas stations, hotels/motels, package express companies, healthcare workers, and others may need to be specially trained in some system of self-defense. This system should be chosen by the company and should adhere to any federal, state, or local policies. The training should be provided at company expense by qualified instructors to avoid any undue liability issues.

Corporate Policy. The risk of violence in the workplace can also be lessened by direct corporate policy in the areas of company regulations, screening procedures during hiring, the utilization of the employees assistance program (EAP), and the fielding of a threat team.

Corporate policies on matters associated with violence should be clearly stated in writing. There should be zero tolerance for weapons on company property whether at work stations or in lockers. Similarly, there should be zero tolerance for the presence of alcohol or drugs on company property. Employees should not drink alcohol two hours before work nor drink alcohol at company functions or during meal times and coffee breaks. To permit otherwise is to court violence unnecessarily.

Employment screening is an effective method of reducing the risk of violence from people for whom the company may be held responsible. Written permission should be obtained from the applicant, and work histories, credit histories, past histories of any felonies, and letters of reference should be examined in detail, but in accordance with any state or local regulations governing these matters. Interviewing notes should be written and kept in personnel files, should the need for such information arise later on.

Although adequate screening can help to rule out problematic employees before they are hired, employee assistance programs can provide training for current employees that further reduces the risk of aggression. Programs for treating substance abuse should be available, but so also should be workshops in verbal conflict resolution, advance technical training, and programs for managers in disciplining, laying off, or terminating employees in humane ways. Attention to these matters avoids unnecessary violent outbursts.

Corporate policy should also dictate the need for a threat team. Companies should have zero tolerance for threats of any type toward anyone. The threat team should be composed of company legal counsel, human resources, and security. This group evaluates all threats by interviewing the recipient of the threat, any employee who may have witnessed the threat, and the person who made the threat. If the individual who made the threat is an employee, all hiring materials should be reviewed as well as any indication of current problems and severe life stress. This information gathering is done in accordance with law, and the threat team, based on its findings, then makes appropriate recommendations for penalties to management. The very fact of a threat team provides a strong nonverbal message to the workforce that such behavior is unacceptable.

The threat team may prove especially helpful to employees who are victims of domestic battering. Such employees should be encouraged to share this information with the company threat team without fear of any corporate reprisal. The threat team can then plan appropriate strategies in house to address the matter should the assailant appear at the worksite. The threat team may also work out appropriate responses with the local police.

Finally, informal corporate policy should foster a buddy system for any high-risk areas on grounds. The most common of these include stairwells, bathrooms, elevators, and parking lots. Employees should be encouraged to pay special attention to these high-risk areas and to go in pairs, if necessary.

These steps for safety are far less expensive than one lawsuit successfully brought against a company, and, along with other socially responsible general business practices, represent a significant contribution by business toward reducing the national increase in violent crime. Owners, managers, employees, customers, and stockholders as well as ordinary citizens can encourage these forms of corporate helpfulness.

Government

The institution of a freely elected government at all levels exists to serve the common good and to provide for the welfare of its citizens by ensuring that they have a reasonable voice in accessing the resources of society needed for everyday life. As with business, government may provide programs to strengthen community as well as to develop specific programs for the various sociological risk factors for violence. This twofold approach, in concert with the initiatives from business and our other societal institutions, further lessens anomie and holds the various risk factors for violent crime to a minimum.

There are hundreds, if not thousands, of programs sponsored by various government agencies, and we can only highlight some of these efforts here. Readers who are employees of federal and state agencies may have opportunities to affect programming at that level. For most, efforts to influence government policy are done at the local, municipal level and in the neighborhoods themselves. These grass roots approaches can be very effective in shaping immediate community needs as well as national policy at a later date. For example, many people agree that the country needs national educational standards to educate our youth for the postindustrial state. While most of us cannot affect national public policy directly, we can start in our own neighborhoods with our own local schools and begin to develop needed standards at home.

Similarly, in our own neighborhoods we can begin to address the problems of violent crime in very simple ways. We can be alert for strangers, and watch out for one another. In like manner, we can begin to think about the government initiatives that we are about to review and to consider how these could be modified and fielded at the community level.

Strengthening Community: Basic Approaches

In an era of international economic competition, the government can protect its citizens and strengthen community in general with policies in four possible areas: protectionism, education and training, public works, and tax policies.

Protectionism refers to restriction imposed by the government on trading with other countries so that they do not have an unfair competitive advantage against our own goods and services. Programs in education and training can reeducate our citizens to be knowledgeable about the latest technological advances so that they remain competitive at home and abroad, when compared to the work forces of other countries. Public works programs are a third intervention that can strengthen community by providing employment for citizens so that locally needed problems are solved, such as having local bridges repaired. Finally, the government can strengthen community by tax policies that transfer income to those in need.

These interventions, if they are employed at various levels of government, need to be thought through adequately. The goal is to strengthen business and communities without disturbing effective business practices and general beneficial principles of free trade among countries. We need our citizens to be members of the postindustrial state and not the permanent underclass. Several observers of the government/business interface (Derber, 1991; Gordon, 1996; Kapstein, 1996; Kortner, 1995; Thurow, 1996) have raised a number of thoughtful approaches to these matters for public discussion and the reader may want to examine these suggestions in greater depth.

There is also the need for public discussion, informed debate, and the emergence of sound public policy on issues that are related to the possible risk factors for violence. These discussions are the responsibility of each of us in our common efforts to reduce violence and strengthen community. Topics include, among others: corporate welfare, campaign financing reform, term limits for office holders, standards for education, gun control, substance abuse, services for victims of untreated PTSD, and privacy issues in technology.

For example, many companies and businesses are provided subsidies and tax breaks that lessen the costs of daily business, but there is no real need for these government benefits. This is known as "corporate welfare." Such benefits may be found in agriculture, energy, timber, manufacturing, and the like, and cost the federal government about one hundred and fifty billion dollars each year. It is in the interest of the country to curtail these unneeded payments, but the process is complicated by political donations from these companies to the country's elected representatives.

The vibrancy of a democracy depends upon the true independence of its legislative bodies to consider the requests and needs of all of its citizens. Solutions need to be determined and compromises need to be reached, but the process should be inherently open to a review of each issue solely on its merits. Theoretically, any citizen should be able to seek elective office, and, if elected, to enter into legislative deliberation with an open mind and a responsivity to the citizens whom the person represents.

However, the process of running for office in our country has become so expensive that those of great wealth can exert undue influence on our elected representatives by contributing vast sums of money to the legislators' re-election campaigns. Such an inherent structural tension exists between business and government. Businesses hire lobbyists whose task is to influence legislation on behalf of business interests and to obtain the government subsidies and tax benefits that we have noted. However, the desires of business (for example, the easing of environmental regulations) may not always be in the best common interest, but the goal of the lobbyist is to prevail in persuading legislators to act in the best interests of business.

One possible solution to this problem of corporate welfare might be the designation of an independent review commission to function as the military-base closure commission did a few years ago. When the Communist threat declined in recent years, the country had more military bases than it needed. Since these bases were located in many states, and provided large payrolls to local states and communities, legislators were reluctant to close bases in their own states. To address the problem, the base closure commission was asked to review these installations, and to make recommendations of which bases should be closed. Congress then had to vote in the affirmative or the negative for the entire list.

A similar process could be used to develop guidelines and limits for all corporate subsidies. A commission would be appointed to devise strategies to curb the inherent structural tension by all business interest groups. Congress would then vote to accept or reject the package. If passed, the new guidelines would have similar applicability at the state and municipal levels.

Discussions such as this are needed for the other topics that we have noted, since these issues and their solutions directly relate to our staying competitive internationally, reducing the size of the permanent underclass, and directly addressing the factors associated with the increased levels of violent crime, which we have documented. The discussion of these matters could begin with neighbors visiting with each other in community meetings at the local school, in the local media as well as in the traditional national, state, and municipal forums for legislative debate. To the extent that individuals participate in the shaping of these policies, they will experience shared values around a common task and anomie will be lessened.

In the interim, government at all levels can begin to formulate more focused policies that strengthen families and, thus, communities. For example, government can work to foster employee corporate ownership in this era of downsizing, to promote employee stock options through tax incentives, to strengthen savings, pension, and retirement plans in the face of dwindling Social Security resources. Many of these initiatives can be addressed locally and in the longer term neighborhoods are strengthened by such programs.

Strengthening Community: Special Areas

As was the case with the business community, various government agencies also have begun programs specifically to address the sociological risk factors that are associated with high levels of violent crime.

The Permanent Underclass. Some state and local governments have taken the initiative in creating business enterprise zones in less affluent neighborhoods such as those in areas of Atlanta and

Detroit. Reduced taxes and the provision of city services such as roads and sewerage linkups make it possible for businesses to hire local residents and to stimulate the local economy through their payrolls.

Government at all levels can foster the education and training of individuals so that they acquire the skills that keep them above the poverty level. Government can provide tax incentives for companies to do this, or they can find programs directly or in cooperation with national charitable foundations. For example, the W. K. Kellogg Foundation has worked with local governments and neighborhood groups to fund a variety of programs for at-risk youth that include mentoring, job training, and church-based support groups. Similarly, the Ford Foundation has fielded an initiative with local governments to reconnect absent fathers with their children by providing needed job training and assistance in obtaining work. The school system in Hartford, Connecticut, is an example of direct government involvement in its own right as it seeks to avoid discrimination in education in providing a quality education to each of its young people. Currently under discussion as possible alternatives are charter schools, magnet schools, school choice, or some form of a voucher system.

There are many other examples of citizen and government involvement that creatively address the issue of the permanent underclass. Eighteen years ago, Dorothy Stoneman decided to help young people gain skills and enhance their self-esteem. Her program, Youthbuild USA, helps teenagers build housing for homeless or low-income citizens and provides them with opportunities for alternative academic and leadership skills. Youthbuild now has one hundred programs in thirty-four states.

Government and the private sector in Louisville, Kentucky, have formed a program to provide students with summer jobs. The students agree to study hard for good grades during the academic year and are promised summer employment in return for their efforts.

With better response times, better building codes, and fire detectors, the fire departments in Miami and Charlotte now use some of their time to clear baseball diamonds, coach students, and provide services for the homeless. The police department in Casselberry, Florida, has a call-back service for the many elderly in the community that they serve. An automated phone service rings elderly residents. If there is no response, the police visit to find out whether the person needs assistance.

Vanderbilt University created a program to meet the needs of aggressive children at high risk to become violent adults. Teachers in Seattle, Washington; Durham, North Carolina; Nashville, Tennessee; and rural Pennsylvania were trained to help the angry children learn to get along with others and share things. There were clear rules and time-outs for aggressive outbursts. Aggressive children in the fourth grade in each of these test cities were compared to aggressive children who were not in the fast-track program. At the end of the program, forty percent of the no-treatment comparison group were in special education classes whereas only twenty-three percent of the intervention group had been assigned to special classes.

Domestic Abuse. Since we have seen how an abused child very often becomes an abusing adult (Widom, 1992), it is important for local government to add to its resources for addressing this important national need. Local governments can be helpful in creating more shelters for battered women and their children, to strengthen local laws that increase the penalties for violating restraining orders, and to foster more active policing of this problem. For example, in this latter case, the police department in Minneapolis, found that the battering of spousal victims ceased if the batterer was arrested rather than being ordered to leave the home for a few hours. Other states in the Midwest have found that coupling the arrest with prosecution by the police department rather than by the frightened spouse results in even greater reductions in subsequent episodes of battering. These approaches along with better risk management strategies for stopping batterers in the workplace can significantly reduce this risk factor. Violence need not breed violence when we have learned how to intervene successfully.

Community Policing. New and improved policing strategies appear to contribute, at least in part, to the declines in violent crime noted in Chapter 1. These include longer prison sentences, a crackdown on illegal guns, gun buy-back plans, the interdiction of illegal drugs, and computerized targeting of high-crime areas. However, an equally important experiment in strengthening community is also taking place within the police community. Known as *community policing*, the goal is to remove officers from patrol cars and have them patrol neighborhoods on foot (or bicycles). The goal is for the officer to get to know the residents of the neighborhood so that trends in violent crime can be identified and solved quickly. This approach addresses several of the risk factors at once, such as substance abuse, domestic violence, hate-based crimes of discrimination, and criminal behavior associated with the permanent underclass. Many police departments nationwide are implementing this approach, and the results have been remarkable.

Consider some of its many examples. In Chicago, the police received a grant for one million dollars to apprehend the city's worst young offenders in gangs. Utilizing racketeering statutes, high-tech wiretaps and money laundering laws, they have been able to arrest thirty-nine gang leaders. Miami, Dallas, Los Angeles, and eleven other cities have received federal monies for similar programs.

In Phoenix, the police have begun neighborhood block watches, antigraffiti campaigns, and the education of children in the school system on safety and crime issues. In Philadelphia, the police meet with community groups to role-play mock arrests in order to avoid community backlashes later on. The Fort Worth police have trained hundreds of citizens for neighborhood patrols and have focused the attention of at-risk youth on recreational activities to keep them from joining gangs. On the theory that criminals commit fewer serious offenses as well as serious crimes, police in New York City have begun enforcing laws on smoking marijuana, shoplifting, and evading subway fares in a crackdown on so-called quality-of-life issues, and it has resulted in a dramatic decrease in serious crime citywide as criminals are stopped for the less serious offenses. Eugene, Oregon, has acquired a state-of-the-art motor vehicle to apprehend drunken drivers.

These mutual efforts are examples of successful interventions to take back the streets from violent criminals. The sense of community is strengthened in the process.

Youth Violence. Most citizens acknowledge that we have a serious problem with youth crime. Less well known is that there are several solutions known to be effective in preventing such violence.

Table 2 outlines these basic approaches. In general, the younger the child is when provided with these helpful interventions, the greater the likelihood of preventing subsequent violence.

An inspection of the items in Table 2 suggests that there are important roles for each of five major institutions in addressing these needs, including those efforts by government. We have seen how business has fielded some helpful initiatives in the areas of academics and social learning, and government has an equally important role. Government may address academics through its school system as we shall see in the next chapter, but it may also provide the leadership in other areas of need.

Local government, in conjunction with the business sector, private foundations, and interested neighborhoods, can field big brother/big sister programs, and foster parent and foster-grand-parent programs. These approaches build caring attachments to isolated youth, and provide tutors, mentors, and role models in acquiring basic academic and social skills. Local governments are in a unique position to sponsor recreational programs and to encourage companies to create summer jobs for students.

Similarly, the municipal community can be of assistance on other matters. Truancy patrols are helpful. Many of our large cities have also found teen curfews to reduce crime and violence, and in twenty-four states 185 teen courts pass judgments on their peers. This last approach has a twofold benefit: peers pass sentences on peers and, thus, adults are not blamed for being unfair; and young people are learning about the law and civic responsibility.

Table 2. Approaches for Preventing Youth Violence

Academics
>Verbal Conflict Resolution
>Vocational Education

Caring Attachments
>Mentors
>Tutors
>Big Brother/Big Sister
>Foster Parents
>Foster Grandparents

Policing
>Curfew
>Teen Courts
>Truancy Patrols

Social Learning
>Summer Jobs
>Recreation Programs

Treatment Interventions
>Child Abuse
>Substance Abuse

Finally, government resources could be directed to provide start-up monies and ongoing funding for programs that address child abuse and substance abuse, factors that at times are both associated with violence. These sociological risk factors greatly enhance the possibility of membership in the permanent underclass and a life of violent crime. Early intervention programs have been shown to be effective, and at present, they are seriously underfunded for those in need of such programs.

FAMILIES

Strengthening Community: Basic Approaches

The family is our basic societal institution for rearing children to be contributing members of society at work, in their own families, and in their neighborhoods. Childrearing is never an easy task in any age and it is more complicated in our own because of the postindustrial shift, values that emphasize self rather than others, and increased levels of violence in society. Rearing children who will not be perpetrators of violence, and who will not themselves be victims of needless violence requires constant vigilance by parents over a period of several years.

Yet, two-career families, working women, and single parents are frequently short of time and long on responsibilities. Work, day care, summer camp, dance recitals, aging parents fill already overcrowded days. Consider the many sacrifices that you must make to accomplish these goals. What to do? Where to begin? How much time to spend on each task?

Because of the importance of parents' being at their best in tasks with their children, this section on families reviews basic issues and solutions facing parents as persons in their own right, and then explores specific childrearing issues in today's age. The family strengthens community and neighborhood when the family fosters mastery, caring attachments, and a meaningful purpose in life for each of its members. The suggestions presented herein are directed toward these goals.

Empowering Parents

Parents today face a number of common problems that may impair their quality of life and make the task of childrearing more difficult. In fact, some of these problems may place that parent and child in harm's way. Included in this list of postindustrial complications are increased life stress, competing value systems for oneself and one's children, parental substance abuse, domestic violence, adequate day care, and parental rights. Resolving these matters first provides parents with more time and energy for their children.

Increased Life Stress. The shifts in the postindustrial state that have resulted in increased competition and increased time-urgency leave many parents overwhelmed and tired out. Since they realize that stressful life problems are better solved when they are at their best, many of today's parents make time to include the basic stress management approach of stress-resistant persons. They understand that the energy invested in a stress management approach yields rich dividends in terms of sustained health and a clarity of mind that saves time in other areas of their lives.

Making time for relaxation periods each day and aerobic exercise each week are two approaches that are powerful means for reducing the physiology of stress, regardless of the particular problems that a person may be facing. Reasonable nutrition and time with other caring persons for support and companionship are similarly helpful in reducing life stress. Taken together, these steps restore energy and provide time to think more clearly about one's daily routine in general, and the task of rearing children in particular.

Competing Values. The postindustrial state has also left parents with two fundamentally different and competing value systems. Choosing the values for one's life and the values to teach one's children are not easy tasks. We have seen how the present primary cultural values of personal entitlement, material acquisition and instant gratification are leading to a callous society, with violence and other lesser forms of harshness. Is the cultural emphasis on power, success, fame, and material acquisition worth the price? The pursuit of these objectives requires a great deal of time and intense competitive pressure with resultant loss of energy and less time for personal and family pursuits. Even successful attainment of these goals frequently leaves the person bored, socially isolated, and lonely. Values that emphasize honesty, trust, responsibility for self and others appear to be better values for oneself and for one's children, and are needed in today's society. However, these are not the major values in society and adhering to them and teaching them to one's children is difficult in the face of the postindustrial cultural pressure. Parents may want to consider the best that each system has to offer (e.g., balancing reasonable material gain with concern for the welfare of others).

Substance Abuse. Parenting is difficult enough without complicating the process further with drugs or alcohol. Substance abuse is inordinately expensive, consumes many hours spent in feeding the addiction, precludes learning better ways to cope, and badly damages caring attachments to children. While heroin, crack/cocaine, and marijuana are frequent parental drugs of choice, alcohol is the most common offender.

Alcoholism is present when one's drinking causes trouble. It is not defined by the type of alcohol consumed or the amount that the person consumes. If one's drinking gets one into trouble, then one is drinking alcoholically. Trouble includes problems with one's boss, spouse, children, physical and mental health, or with the law. In our clinics we often ask a person four questions about alcohol: (1) Do you need an eye-opener? (2) Do you get angry when people discuss alcohol? (3) Has anyone ever told you to cut back on your consumption? (4) Do you feel guilty?

An answer of yes to two or more of these questions indicates problems with alcohol abuse. There are good treatments for both drug and alcohol abuse, and parents may wish to avail themselves of these opportunities to free themselves from this unnecessary life stress.

Domestic Violence. In a similar way, neither parents nor children deserve to be victims of violence. Nor is this violence more tolerable if the children are only witnesses to the violence. We should note that one can be psychologically traumatized equally by being a victim or by witnessing violent acts happening to others.

If one is a victim of spousal violence, there is help and there is no embarrassment in seeking it. Many police departments now have domestic violence units, and officers in many states are now required to arrest batterers. Many communities have shelters for battered women that provide safety and protection, and where children may accompany their mothers. Emergency rooms of hospitals, mental health counselors, family attorneys, and the clergy are all possible resources with which to begin.

If one is a single parent who is feeling overwhelmed and begins to abuse her children, parental abuse hotlines, mental health counselors, clergy, other parents, and other friends or relatives can be helpful in assisting that parent to gather needed support as well as better training in the parenting skills needed to solve problems in nonviolent ways.

Hawaii has an exemplary program in this regard. Hawaii Healthy Start is a social service program that screens all new mothers at the birth of their children. In particular, the staff is looking for mothers who are overwhelmed due to domestic violence, substance abuse, no prenatal care, or an attempted abortion of the new child. A family helper is assigned to the parent for five years. During this time, the parent has a support network and is taught how to reward and punish children safely, how to stimulate a child's curiosity, and the like. This program has reported sharp reductions in subsequent child abuse and there are now two hundred similar programs in thirty states.

The principle for success is clear: if one is feeling overwhelmed and abusive, there are many resources for support and help in learning parenting skills. Some abused parents believe that they cannot change, but the experience of those of us who counsel in a variety of settings is that this perception is inaccurate.

Day Care. Adequate day care is another important issue for today's parents and can be a source of great concern for parents. Parental work responsibilities frequently entail placing children in day care, and parents understandably want the best placement for their children. Some day care is provided by business for their employees, some by private agencies, some by public agencies, and some by extended families. Sometimes, groups of parents band together and rotate childrearing responsibilities when other alternatives are not available.

Recent findings by the National Institute of Child Health and Human Development have provided some encouraging results. This ten-site longitudinal study of 1,300 children has found no apparent negative effects on the development of caring attachments to parents in the first fifteen months of life. Some disrupted attachments were found in mothers who were insensitive or unresponsive to their children and who were anxious or depressed, but these disruptions appeared to be more a function of the parent's make-up than the day care setting itself.

While this is encouraging, it is still true that studies of day care placement are new and evolving. Several studies suggest that good day care programs teach the child excellent cognitive skills, but that social skills and feelings need to be strengthened by parents. A further concern is the lack of uniform standards for settings, staffing, and programmatic settings, but there are good day care settings and parents may want to leave time to assess several before making their choice.

Parental Rights. A final issue of common concern is the role of parental rights. In a society that emphasizes personal advancement and material gain, many of the responsibilities of parents have fallen to other social institutions such as the schools and government agencies, and many parents are not comfortable with what their children are being taught and how parents are being held responsible for the wayward behavior of their children.

A couple in Michigan was recently fined for their son's delinquent behavior. Another couple found that their third grade child was referred to counseling that they felt was not in the best interest of their child. Neither the school nor the courts would honor the parents' request to stop the counseling. Whereas states already have laws against parental child abuse and contributing to the delinquency of minors, about fifteen states have added additional parental liability laws to hold parents accountable for rearing their children properly.

Although some parents advocate for a congressional parental rights amendment that would protect the fundamental right of a parent to direct the upbringing of a child, these matters are difficult to legislate in practice. A more workable solution may lie in parents' reassertion of their moral authority over their children and working closely and cooperatively with schools and government agencies to find acceptable solutions to the children's needs.

This concerned interest by the adult community enhances caring attachments to children, provides a set of coherent moral guidelines, and, in time, strengthens community—with the risk for violence also declining.

Issues in Childrearing

As we have noted, the goal of childrearing is to nurture children who become happy, productive, nonviolent adults. Creating reasonable mastery, caring attachments, and a meaningful purpose in life while avoiding as much as possible the sociological risk factors for violence are key factors in this process, and our discussion will focus on these domains. Since disrupted caring attachments are so fundamental in violence, we begin our discussion there.

Caring Attachments. Adequate caring attachments have several components and include spending time with the child, teaching the child how to trust others, instilling empathy, and developing adequate self-esteem.

Children find the presence of adults protective and comforting. Children need time to think, ask questions, try out solutions, ask for feedback and direction, and so forth. All of this takes adult time. Our public swimming pools, movie theaters, and public libraries are filled with children who are in need of more contact with their parents. For caring attachments to take root, children need time and attention in the physical presence of their parents.

Next, children need to learn how to trust. This is not guesswork or a feeling one has. Trust is composed of predictable behavior and similar values of concern for others. Predictable behavior means that what a person says that person will do is actually done. If the teacher promises to be in class each day at eight o'clock in the morning, and the teacher is there each day, then the teacher's behavior is predictable to the students. Since the world is a complicated place for all of us, we are given some leeway for making errors and not doing what we have said that we will do. As long as we have some reasonable explanation for these infrequent lapses, our behavior is considered predictable.

For this predictable behavior to be considered trustworthy, the second element of similar values of concern for others must be present in each party. Behavior that we can rely on must be motivated by honesty, support, and concern for one another. If someone values stealing and mayhem, one may be able to predict that person's deviant behavior, but that person would not be considered trustworthy. Young children, particularly as they get older, can be taught this skill by assignments to observe the behavior and values of others and themselves, and then to report on the results.

A third component of developing caring attachments consists in teaching the child to have empathy and tolerance for others. Parents instill this skill by teaching children the correct labels for various feelings, by teaching the child when the child is experiencing these feelings and why these feelings are occurring, and then in going the next step and teaching the child when others have similar feelings and the reasons for why they are experiencing them. Feelings of joy, happiness, and excitement need to be learned and empathetically understood in others, along with the feelings of anger, guilt, sadness, and hurt. Children can practice empathy by considering how their pets, their siblings, their parents, and their friends may be feeling about a particular event. This process requires considerable feedback on the part of parents before it is mastered, but it is central to developing lifelong skills in understanding others and being tolerant of differences. Training in empathy early on decreases the probability of discrimination in later adult life.

A fourth component in caring attachments is accurate self-esteem. Adequate self-esteem is built on a true evaluation of a person's strengths and weaknesses, an adequate assessment of their responsibilities and rights. The events in a child's day are best evaluated individually. The child is told that he or she was good for putting away the toys and walking a brother across the street. The child is told that he or she was not good for stealing the extra cookies and not taking a bath. The child is told that he or she needs to develop better skills at riding the bicycle by means of more practice. This form of specifically referenced appraisal helps the child learn what the child does well and where more effort for growth is needed. Generalized statements without referents, such as "Tommy is a good boy," are of little help, and statements such as "you are just like your father" are not accurate and may confuse the child.

Mastery. While parents are developing and refining these attachment skills, they can also begin the work of developing reasonable mastery in their children. Children need to learn to shape the world to meet their needs, and are helped by parents who find a balance between encouraging independence and providing support during the learning periods. Sooner or later, the parent will not be present and the child will need to be able to cope alone. The scientific research indicates that children do best when attempting to do things by themselves with appropriate cognitive direction, emotional support, and guidance from the parents. This process of learning to master responsibility for self-care, care of property, and the care of others is greatly advanced if parents break each task into small manageable steps. The child's growth is further enhanced if the child develops the characteristics utilized by stress-resistant persons for managing stress and anger: good problem-solving skills, healthy lifestyle choices in diet and exercise, and the use of humor. The use of aerobic exercise also helps to reduce the potential for aggression, as recreation programs for at-risk youth across the country have demonstrated.

As children learn to master various specific tasks, they will also be able to develop a sense of personal responsibility. Businessperson Nancy Godfred (1995) has written a helpful book to teach children about responsibility. For example, when children begin to earn money, the family could have a citizen-of-the-household tax jar and a charity tax jar into which the child is expected to place a small percentage of the child's earnings. The child helps to decide how to spend the tax and charitable monies collected by all of the family's members. This simple procedure teaches children about civic responsibility as well as concern for the less fortunate. Her book contains many similar and helpful suggestions.

The child's sense of mastery is also enhanced with training in the more complex social and academic skills. Children need to learn to respect views and choices of others, to learn the basic social graces, to learn verbal conflict resolution skills for addressing the inevitable differences of opinion over life's many issues, and to have zero tolerance for weapons and for violence, except in cases of self-defense in the face of imminent harm. In these latter situations, children need to be taught when it is a matter of self-defense and how to deal with the bully.

Today's parents will also want to be active in overseeing the growth of their child's academic skills. Has the child learned the basics of English, math, and computer science? Is the child taking courses that will leave the child prepared for gainful employment in our postindustrial knowledge-based society? Does the child understand money matters, including banking and credit? Seeing that homework is done, participating closely with teachers, and being acquainted with the child's school friends are additional ways in which parents can enhance the mastery skills of their children.

Parents have developed some creative ways of teaching a variety of basic mastery skills. North Carolina and Georgia have mobilized local citizens in statewide efforts to combat the rise of teenage pregnancies. With public education and community outreach, the levels of teenage pregnancies have begun to decline. A hospital in New York City uses its waiting room for reading to children and teaching parenting skills to parents as the family waits for medical care. Seattle citizens address the anger in at-risk youth for violence by sponsoring the Seattle Summer Young Writer's Workshop. The program is teaching alternative ways to express anger without resorting to violence and has proven its value.

The National Task Force on African American Males sponsored by the Kellogg Foundation in 1992 developed several suggestions for black youth. Among other things, these included encouraging business development, requiring that school be year-round, developing a network of black-youth camps for recreation, and putting emphasis on education and the use of libraries. To address underage teenage alcohol abuse when driving, the citizens of thirty-four states have passed some sort of legislation that automatically suspends the license of a minor who is driving a car with any amount of alcohol in the minor's bloodstream. Their efforts in this regard have become a model for similar federal legislation.

Meaningful Purpose. A meaningful purpose in life is the third domain for parental consideration. The medical and scientific findings suggest that children are best served when they have a balance between reasonable ambition and a sense of responsibility toward others. The Declaration of Independence, the great religions of the world, and the characteristics of stress-resistant persons all emphasize concern for others as an integral part of developing a meaningful purpose in life. Values such as honesty, trustworthiness, being responsible, respecting the rights of others, and being concerned for the welfare of others appear to be in the long-term best interest of the child and of society.

Research shows us that children will learn these values best if they have clear definitions of what behaviors are acceptable and not acceptable, and what rewards or penalties should be expected. Children will learn these values correctly if discipline for unacceptable behaviors is consistent.

In addition to teaching these values directly, parents enhance their children's learning by role-modeling adult behavior that espouses these same values. Just as children learn to be aggressive through a social modeling learning process, they can also learn more pro-social behaviors. For additional values training, some parents have chosen to have their children attend religious observances or to enroll their child in a private school system that espouses values consistent with the parents' beliefs.

Being a volunteer is another excellent way to teach children compassion for others. A recent Gallup Poll for the Independent Sector, a coalition of volunteer groups in Metairie, Louisiana, indicated that about 90 million Americans volunteer around 19.5 billion hours of service for a dollar equivalent of $182 billion dollars. This is still a remarkable strength of our country; children should be encouraged to join in.

Children and teenagers may also be encouraged to volunteer to help the sick, the elderly, the homeless, and the like, or volunteer for causes such as protecting the environment or banning nuclear waste. Projects can be tapped for local need. For example, Mississippi has started a volunteer teacher corps, and recruits college graduates to volunteer to teach underprivileged for a year or two in return for a small stipend. The possibilities are endless and there are many local programs in need of such volunteer services to foster caring attachments and to strengthen the sense of community in local neighborhoods.

Strengthening Community: Special Areas

To close our section on childrearing and violent behavior, we turn to three issues of special importance to parents: (1) substance abuse, (2) depression and suicidal thoughts that often accompany depression, and (3) the influence of the media.

Substance Abuse. Table 3 includes some of the more common warning signs of substance abuse. Teenage behavior is often inconsistent as the young adult tries new roles and new ways of coping, and some of the signs in Table 3 may be due to normal teen growth (for example, being depressed or not getting enough sleep). Some of the signs in Table 3 may also be due to medical illness, bereavement, and the side effects of prescribed medication, to name a few.

Table 3. Drug Abuse: Some Possible Warning Signs

Body Physiology	*Feeling States*
Decreased Alertness	Depression
Loss of Appetite	Elation
Shallow Breathing	Hostility
Drowsiness	Irritability
Glazed Eyes	
Loss of Libido	*Behaviors*
Poor Motor Coordination	Appears Intoxicated
Dilated Pupils	Dark Glasses
Disturbed Sleep	Drug Paraphernalia
Slurred Speech	Long-Sleeve Shirts or Blouses
	(to hide needle marks)

Thus, the signs in Table 3 are best considered as possible warnings, particularly if their appearance is sudden or occurs over a protracted period of time. If you are concerned, it is helpful to tell your child or adolescent of those concerns in a nonaccusatory manner, and to insist that these symptoms be evaluated by your family physician to rule out substance abuse or other serious illness. Parents will want to be particularly alert to alcohol abuse. Two in ten teenagers are addicted to alcohol and, since alcohol is usually the least expensive and most readily available drug, it is consumed more frequently. Violent deaths due to teenage drunk driving are at unacceptable levels; they devastate families and communities. If you find your child abusing drugs or alcohol, a variety of helpful treatment programs are available locally. Call the family physician or local hospital emergency room for information on where to begin.

Depression. Our country is also dealing with unacceptably high levels of adolescent depression and suicide, estimated by some accounts to be occurring nationally at the rate of one every fifty-nine minutes. Again, families and whole communities are impacted.

Table 4 presents some common signs of depression. As with the signs of possible drug abuse, these signs can be due to actual bereavement or some other major loss (for example one's job or one's home in a natural disaster), to untreated psychological trauma or PTSD, to serious medical illnesses, and, again, to the side effects of some medications. As with the signs of substance abuse in Table 1, the signs of possible depression in Table 4 are to be treated with equal seriousness. Ask the child or adolescent if he or she is feeling depressed and suicidal. Have a young person with the signs in Table 4 see the family physician immediately. There are good treatments for depression in adolescents and for any suicidal thoughts or plans that may accompany such depression.

The Media. Finally, parents will want to monitor the impact of the media on their children's growth in these violent times. While the government can develop national policies to curtail violence and while the industry can attempt to police itself, there is no substitute for parental supervision. Teach your child to be media literate by helping your child understand the meaning of the programming. What does the violence mean, what does it do to the victims, and what are alternatives to resolving the problem in nonviolent ways? Parents may also want to come together in advocacy groups to influence governmental policy, to organize

Table 4. Depression: Some Possible Warning Signs

Poor Appetite
Poor Concentration
Depressed Mood
Feelings of Guilt
Feelings of Hopelessness
Loss of Libido
Diminished Sense of Pleasures
Sleep Disturbances
Suicidal Thought or Plans
Weight Loss
Worthlessness/Low Self-Esteem

boycotts and the like, but day-to-day monitoring and correcting the false messages is truly necessary.

This section has outlined basic parental and childrearing considerations for the early childhood development of decent children who are socially adept, intellectually curious, and not predisposed to violence. Although some of these tasks are familiar, we do not want to underestimate their importance. As familiar as they are, the statistics on youth crime (Chapter 5) suggest that many children still have not mastered these basic academic and social skills.

SCHOOLS

Strengthening Community: Basic Approaches

Society looks to its schools to strengthen the development of the child that has begun at home so that our young people mature into productive, socially responsible citizens. Time and again we have noted the importance of education in the postindustrial state. Education is important to all of us in terms of our national strength in a competitive global economy as well as to us individually in terms of adequate employment and a decent quality of life for our children and our grandchildren. As long as children in other parts of the world are better educated than our own citizens, earned income will reside in those other countries, the permanent underclass will continue to grow at home, and we can expect violence and crime to persist. As a nation, it is in our interest to address the issues related to adequate schooling. We need to draw upon the resources of administrators, teachers, teachers' unions, parents, and citizens who may no longer have school-age children as we attempt to improve our national quality of education.

Standards. There are many possible ways to strengthen ourselves academically. The first is to pool our created energies and resources in developing curricula that are tailored to the needs of the emerging knowledge-based state and the service system needed to support it. We need to move beyond the Taylor curriculum that trains students for industrial jobs that no longer exist, and focus on courses that teach computer literacy and the intellectual skills needed for the analytic thinking required for research and development.

The development of national standards is a second approach that many are considering. The standards would contain a basic minimum level of educational attainment, and would require that no student be allowed to graduate until that student has mastered the basic skills needed to be a productive citizen. Some states such as Arkansas, Louisiana, North Carolina, South Carolina, and Virginia already have promotional exams of some form. The country could follow these examples and develop national exams for elementary, middle, and high schools as other countries do. These exams might contain different standards for those bound for college versus those bound for vocational and trade careers, but either would address the need for some minimum standard of competence for each citizen.

A third method of improving academic excellence being considered by several states is the use of a parent voucher system. A school district determines how much money is allotted for the education of each child. The parent is then given a voucher for that dollar amount, and can choose which school his or her child should attend. Various proposals include choices of public schools, religious schools, private schools, or some combination of these groupings. This approach is meant to reward good schools and to introduce some element of competition into the education system on the assumption that this will increase the overall level of quality over time. Although this approach has some merit, consideration needs to be given to those children who may remain in the less adequate school programs. Without adequate resources, the possibility of learning the basic skills needed for the postindustrial state is reduced. Both they as individuals and society as a whole will not benefit if they graduate into the permanent underclass.

A fourth possible approach to improving academic standards is to encourage business, colleges, and universities to become actively involved in improving the quality of education in local public schools. These organizations can be helpful in providing faculty to enhance the education of the classroom teachers and even to teach courses directly. Their presence enhances interest in the real world of business and employment or provides incentive motivation for higher education.

These suggestions are by no means exhaustive of the possibilities, and other creative solutions are being fielded. What is common to all of these approaches is an awareness of the importance of some basic standard of academic attainment for our children.

Physical Plant and Supplies. Students cannot be expected to do their best work in facilities that are unsafe and that lack basic resources. Although many affluent suburbs have adequate resources, many more urban, suburban, and rural settings do not. The problem is further complicated by a growing reluctance of the citizenry to provide extra school funding requests by means of increased taxes.

Since dollars are scarce, basic business practices of fiscal awareness may be of value to school systems. Here the private business sector might provide needed expertise in advising principals and school boards in sound financial planning. In addition, the private sector might also provide some form of direct financial assistance. Consider the following example. The Harriet Tubman School is located in a low-income neighborhood of Newark, New Jersey, but its students excel academically. Much of this has been accomplished with money from private foundations. Over the years, these funds have been used to train parents in how to read to their children; to purchase computers, science, and video equipment for academics; and to provide musical instruments for social and recreational purposes. This is a good example of the potentially creative solutions from the public education/private foundation interface.

Teachers. Teachers are clearly pivotal figures in our collective efforts to improve the quality of education nationally. Teachers have a complicated mission, and deserve the support of all of us in a variety of ways to ensure their success.

To begin with, it seems unreasonable to expect teachers to perform all of the social roles that we noted earlier. Although many attempt in good faith to be parental surrogates, nurses, policemen and the like, these other roles take time from the basic mission of teaching and creative thinking is needed on how to free teachers from these nonacademic roles. Greater parental involvement, adult volunteers, and the emerging role of the school as a one-step health delivery system (see below) are all helpful beginnings in this regard.

Teachers also need our assistance in strengthening their academic roles. This includes time to prepare relevant curricula and to maintain proficiency in their subject area, and school systems have developed a number of creative ways to provide teachers with these opportunities for continuing education in this era of rapid postindustrial change. These academic efforts are greatly enhanced if the school system has adopted policies that foster learning. Policies of zero tolerance for weapons, for substance abuse, and for violence in the building or on school grounds enable teachers and students to feel safe and then to concentrate on academic matters.

Academics. The academic deficiencies that we have noted earlier suggest the need for students in the postindustrial period to have a thorough grounding in English, math, general science, and computer literacy. A working knowledge of literature and history are also helpful to students as these bodies of knowledge show us how people deal with pain, suffering, and death; how societies prevent people from behaving in aggressive and greedy ways; and how these same societies utilize law and morality to enhance the meaning of life. These subjects teach the student to make informed choices, an important skill in the knowledge-based society.

Schools are developing creative solutions to enhance academics for the knowledge-based society. Some states like Georgia, South Carolina, and Texas have begun to emphasize early childhood education at the preschool level for children at risk and have developed a variety of programs to teach basic academic and social skills. Georgia has gone one step further and provides free preschool education to all of its four-year-olds. Early results are encouraging. For example, those who have been in the preschool program in Georgia score higher academically than those without schooling.

Other programs have been developed to meet the needs of older students. For example, based on the assumption that the school is the hub of its communities, Chicago opens two-thirds of its public schools for the summer. Summer programs include academics, art, music, tutoring, and recreational programs. This is a creative approach to the needs of students in the summer and also increases the total number of school days spent in preparation for the postindustrial economy.

Schools have approached the problem of declining parental involvement in recent years in equally creative ways. Some school districts have parent advisory boards for hiring, curriculum development, and drafting policies on violence and drugs and other school matters. In this way, parents have a voice in their children's academic needs. For example, parents have been a force in creating alternative schools to ensure that students receive an adequate education. Maine now has the Maine School of Science and Math for junior and senior high school students who wish to specialize in these areas. Chelsea, Massachusetts, parents joined with the faculty from Boston University in creating an intergenerational reading program. In this joint effort, parents keep a portfolio of what their children read, and the faculty help parents teach their children the skills of understanding the setting, problem, solutions, and consequences of each story. In the Williamsburg section of Brooklyn, New York, when the drop-out rate became unacceptably high, the community created the El Puente Academy for Peace and Justice to reach out to students from a different cultural background. These examples of constructive parental involvement channel creative parental energies into traditional school programs with beneficial outcomes for the students and their families.

After School. Since most juvenile violent crime occurs after school, the community benefits if its school do not remain closed at the end of the school day. These buildings are potentially an important community resource for addressing the needs of our youth and for curbing violence.

When school is not in session, the school provides a community locale and set of resources for needed community activities. Recreational programs can be conducted for youth. Drop-in centers can be created to provide social support to substance abusers in treatment, for single mothers needing training in parental skills, for support and retraining for laid-off adult employees, for senior citizens, for youth to hang out and the like. These programs are not meant to provide additional responsibilities for teachers and would be run by specialists in each area of need.

Health care provides an interesting example of the school's potential as a resource. Health care reform with its recent emphasis on the highest quality of care in the most cost-effective setting has led to service integration in many health care settings. A similar need to cut costs in education settings is leading to the emergence of a school-based one-stop health care delivery center. In one school setting, children and their parents can address academic needs, physical and mental health needs, substance abuse treatment, and a variety of social services from a team of specialists already on site.

Consider these examples. In Memphis, counseling, substance abuse treatment, social services consultations as well as curriculum development, educational programs, and psychosocial evaluations can now be obtained in one stop at school. Texas is starting its "Schools of the Future" program, which integrates health and human services with educational needs. Active involvement of parents, teachers, and public and private community organizations is expected. In Kentucky, when the state legislature reformed educational standards statewide, it also provided for the development of school-based Family Resources and Youth Services Centers. These centers can provide resources to families for coping with life stress, serious mental illness, substance abuse, and other needed social services.

These one-stop school-based health and social service programs provide needed resources and ease of access to parents who are busy and feeling overwhelmed, and they also provide a potential solution to the current problem of multiple roles for teachers. As resources become available in the school itself, students can be referred as need dictates. In this way, the school has become an important resource for each set of stakeholders, and augments the sense of community.

Strengthening Community: Special Areas

In addition to teaching academics, schools need to further enhance the social skills of our young people and there are at least three sociological risk factors which could be actively addressed within the school community: substance abuse, weapons and violence, and discrimination.

Substance Abuse. Young people see drugs being bought and sold on the street and in their playgrounds and they have little information with which to make reasonable judgments. Children and adolescents need courses on drugs and what they can do to the body and one's ability to work and enjoy life. The message on the street is one of glamour, not of physical pain and violence. Although students need to learn to say NO, they also need to learn a set of verbal and behavioral skills that enable them to say NO in the face of considerable social pressure from drug dealers and peers. Role-playing how to say no with the skills necessary to implement this solution is one school approach that has proved helpful in many states.

Violence. School programs have also been developed to address violent behavior in its many forms. Many students do not feel safe in coming to school or in being in the building itself. Some even bring guns for self-defense, which only compounds the problem. Metal detectors and security guards may help, but the presence of potentially violent students induces fear in many nonviolent youngsters and interferes with academic learning. School districts may wish to consider policies where the chronically violent students are educated in a separate setting.

School materials that present information on what violence is, what are the types of violence, what causes violence to escalate, its warning signs, and what can be done to de-escalate aggression before it occurs, are helpful. Such a curriculum provides the teacher with the opportunity to teach verbal conflict resolution skills, the difference between being assertive (stating clearly your needs in a way that invites cooperation) and being aggressive (attempting to fulfill your own needs at the expense of others by force or fraud), and to refine empathic skills. [See Hechinger (1994) for a recent review of effective programs in this regard.]

Discrimination. Finally, sensitivity training for understanding, appreciating, and tolerating the differences in others is an additional area where school training may be helpful. Helping students understand differences in terms of race, ethnicity, religion, gender, age, or physical hardship as well as what we all have in common reduces the fear of the unknown and enhances more cooperative behavior in the long term. Such training early on at home and reinforced in school reduces the risk of scapegoating a group of people when times are difficult and resources are scarce, and may enhance group cohesiveness of all the members in the face of life stress.

Religion

Religion has always been a central force in our country, but how are we to understand its place in an era of scientific advancement and the emergence of the postindustrial state that is built upon scientific advances? A brief explanation may be of help as we contemplate our technological advances.

Overview. In 1901–2, psychologist William James (1958) gave a series of lectures on religion at the University of Edinburgh in Scotland. Surveying the variety of possible religious experiences, he came to the following conclusions. First, he believed that the evidence showed that the visible, physical world is part of a larger spiritual universe. Second, he felt that union or harmony with that spiritual universe was the true goal of our life's activities and that this yearning was biologically rooted. Third, he stated that prayer was the pathway from this physical world to the spiritual universe. His studies and observations suggested to him that religious people had a new zest for life, and that religion provided believers with a sense of security, peace, and love for others. He was adamant in insisting that there were needs for differing religions, in that each people's histories and problems differed, but he was equally firm in the belief that science could not fill the void of religious experience because science dealt with the abstract and concrete whereas religion dealt with the personal aspects of experience.

Historians Will and Ariel Durant similarly have much to teach about the role of religion in a society such as ours. After having written several volumes that encompassed ten thousand years of human history, they wrote a small volume that distilled the lessons from history that they had learned (1968). Both morals and religion were considered.

Morals are the rules by which a society exhorts its members to behave so that the social order is preserved. As with William James, the Durants found that there were universal moral ethics that were altered at times by history and the environment. For example, the hunter-gatherers emphasized brutality, bellicosity, and sexual readiness to survive. This was replaced during the agricultural period of human history by the values of industriousness, thrift, and peace. During the industrial revolution, individualism and material gain again rose to the fore.

Religion emerges when these codes of morals are received from God. The belief in religion helps people who are suffering and are unhappy. It helps the bereaved. It gives dignity to the poor and disabled. It provides discipline for the young, and it can make human relationships sacred as it does in matrimony. Religion not only helps us understand joy, but it provides meaning in the face of pain, suffering, and death, issues over which science provides little solace.

The Durants came to conclusions similar to those of William James. Religion is important to society in that in all of history there is no significant example of a society maintaining an adequate moral order without religion. The differing needs of people require flexibility in the religious experience but science will never be an adequate substitute.

The Durants provide two additional lessons from history that are important in our own immediate age: (1) religion must prevail when laws are weak and the moral resolve of the people must maintain the social order and (2) war increases the moral laxity of any age.

Thus, the answer to our question is that religion does have an important role to play in an age of science. Its role takes on additional importance when we consider that ours is an age of enormous change based on technological advances and an age that has seen its share of wars.

That our understanding of religion is changing and evolving should neither surprise nor frighten us. Change in religion is part of American history. The colonial state churches gave rise to several Protestant denominations which in turn grew into a variety of religious experiences and faiths. In our current periods of change, the challenge is to retain the basic message of all of the world's great religions: a sacred concern for the welfare of others. Ernest Becker (1973) was correct when he cited a person's need to find transcendent meaning as a way of addressing one's own mortality. Concern for others was his suggestion for transcendence and remains an important goal for religion, and for believers in an age of crime and violence.

Clergy. The American Psychological Association recently reported on a survey of today's clergy. There were 225,000 Protestant ministers, 4,000 rabbis, and 53,000 Catholic priests. These clergy spend ten to twenty percent of their time in counseling activities for an estimated 148.2 million hours of counseling a year. Not included in the survey were clergy of other faiths and about 100,000 Roman Catholic nuns. Clearly, here is a powerful moral voice for society.

Their counseling activities include working with the young, preparing couples for marriage and parenting, visiting the sick and the disabled, consoling the dying and the bereaved, and working on community tasks to strengthen society. In each of these activities, the clerical voice can begin to foster caring attachments and strengthen community by addressing the moral decay and violence in society.

Religious Format. Sociologist Robert Wurthnow (1994) has documented the gradual emergence of a new form of worship, the small group. Four out of ten Americans now belong to a small group and many are in religious settings. Bible-study classes, the treatment of addictions, singles and divorced groups, parenting groups, educational and recreation groups for youth are methods being adopted by many of our citizens as a way of attaining a sense of individual belonging, emotional support, and companionship. It is as if society is developing its own new capacity to generate caring attachments and a sense of community in the face of the disruptions that have recently been encountered.

Strengthening Community: Basic Approaches and Special Areas

Sustained by concern for others and working within the small-group format, the clergy are at work on many exciting projects that address the need for community as well as specific sociological risk factors. Following are some examples.

Since 1917, Father Flanagan's Boy's Town has been taking care of children in need. Expanding beyond its initial vision, the program now takes children of both genders and all creeds, races, and ethnic groups. It is family oriented in small residential homes, and includes emerging shelters and a national research hospital. Its focus for over 17,000 children has been and remains that of discipline, family, skills-based education, and religion.

Brandeis University has just completed its tenth year of a summer institute for teachers that instructs them in an antidiscrimination curriculum. Over 25,000 teachers have attended. In June of 1995, the Southern Baptist Convention, which broke away from the American Baptist Convention in defense of slavery over 150 years ago, formally renounced racism in any form.

Campus Ministries at Columbia University, Vanderbilt University, Boston University, and the University of Southern California, to name a few, have all strengthened their programs in response to university student demand. Mission Mississippi, funded by sixty local churches and major state-based corporations, has begun a racial program statewide to reduce discrimination and hatred.

Islam has begun several initiatives nationally. For example, in the East Germantown neighborhood of Philadelphia a mosque opened in 1992 that offers home-work associations, crime watches, a Big Brother program, and classes in computer programming and typing. Another recent religious development has been the growth of the megachurches, such as that of Las Colinas in Irving, Texas. These churches may have anywhere from 3,000 to 15,000 members, but the emphasis is on an array of small groups to make members of the congregations feel part of the community.

More recently, many churches have also become very active in economic issues in pressing for workers' rights. Banding together with labor unions and community development groups, they have begun to address the needs of the permanent underclass by seeking just wages at a poultry-processing plant in North Carolina, in starting an employee-owned health care company in Connecticut, and in assisting employees in buying firms close to bankruptcy in Massachusetts.

As with parenting and schools, there are as many potential creative solutions as there are clergy who undertake them. This chapter clearly indicates that the family, school, and religion remain powerful moral voices in which ordinary citizens and groups of citizens are making strides in containing violence and crime.

Violence in America: Some Final Thoughts

We have seen how periods of great social change, such as the one we are now experiencing in the postindustrial state, require our major societal institutions (business, government, the family, school, and religion) to change and that the guidelines for acceptable behavior from these institutions change as the institutions themselves are altered. Caring attachments are disrupted, the sense of community is weakened, and anomie is pervasive. During such a period, the other risk factors for violence are exacerbated. In our own age we are seeing increased biological risk factors in hyperreactive states, increased sociological risk factors in poverty, domestic violence, discrimination, inadequate schooling, substance abuse, and violence in the media, and increased psychological risk factors in faulty mastery and faulty meaning based on injustice and evil choices.

However, we have also learned that we are not helpless in the face of this national public health problem, that we are not a "traumatized society" as some would suggest. We have seen an array of approaches by ordinary citizens and professionals that contain and reduce violence by strengthening caring attachments and the sense of community as well as by addressing specific sociological risk factors. Just as the risk factors can contribute individually and interactively to increased crime, the remedial intervention of citizens individually and collectively can decrease crime. Americans have been successful with this problem in the past, and we can be so again.

Some will say that this will not be easy. This is true. People who are violent and commit crimes will not quickly stop. It will require the persistent efforts of each of us to strengthen the moral voice of concern for others in our societal institutions.

Some will say that we should start with the very young. This is true. The sooner we create caring attachments for the country's children, and teach them that rights carry with them responsibilities toward others, the more quickly will societal violence subside.

Some will say that this is hard to do alone. This is also true. None of us can solve this problem alone. We need to choose an area to address that is consistent with our skills and interests and then seek out others who have the same concerns. In this process, we shall be forming small groups and developing with each other the caring attachments that strengthen our communities and minimize the negative effects of anomie.

Some will say that ours is an age of cynicism and that citizens will not come forward. This is not true. Even in an age of personal entitlement, there remain citizens who want to help others. Each week presents examples of such men and women participating in neighborhood environmental clean-ups, engaging in walks and marathons for special charities, serving meals to the elderly and homeless, and so forth. The volunteer spirit in America remains. The desire for community is present.

Initiatives now exist to reduce violent crime. A lasting tragedy would occur if the information in these pages was not put to use. Many of us have an understandable reluctance to become involved or the desire to leave it to the next person. The result of these approaches will be a continuing spiral of crime and violence. A better strategy is for each of us to invest our energies in one small, manageable aspect of the problem. This personal commitment by each of us will ultimately reduce the violence in our homes, in our worksites, and in our communities.

The challenge to create communities that are safe and responsive, for ourselves and for our children, is before us. Together, let us take back the night.

(Flannery, R. B. Jr. *Violence in America: Coping with Drugs, Distressed Families, Inadequate Schooling, and Acts of Hate.* Riverdale, NY: American Mental Health Foundation, 2012. Chapters 5 and 6.)

FIVE

Preventing Youth Violence

And in today, already walks tomorrow.
—Samuel Taylor Coolidge

Love bears all things.
—I Corinthians 13:7

He stopped the car, thought for a moment, and then got out. He felt uneasy, but he walked over anyway.

"Hi, mother. I told you that I'd be back to visit. It's been a while, and, even though it is still difficult for me, I am here to be with you.

"I want to begin by apologizing for that period in my life when I caused you so much sorrow. I regret that we argued so much, that I stole money from your purse, and that I got drunk more times that I can count. I know now that it was a difficult time for me, but I am still saddened at the pain that I caused everyone in the family. Since words don't come easily to me, I have written a short poem to express my thanks to you. Let me read it now.

> *"I was consumed with rage,*
> *and you calmed me.*
> *I felt like damaged goods,*
> *and you valued me.*
> *I wanted to destroy myself,*
> *and you protected me.*

I was filled with self-hate,
   and you loved me.
Thank you for being there."
   With that, on this cold February morning, the seventh
anniversary of her death, her foster son knelt down gently,
and placed his poem and a single red rose on the grave site of
the woman who had taken him in and saved his life from a
violent end.
   Even after seven years, the snow associated with her death
still fell heavy on his heart.

As this vignette suggests, troubled youth can be helped before
violence has run its course. There are remedies and interventions
that are helpful. However, this example also demonstrates that
addressing these matters does not necessarily run smoothly, and
that perseverance on the part of the child and the parent, teacher,
or counselor is necessary.

Preventing youth violence by addressing the needs of individuals is best understood as part of a more comprehensive approach
to youth violence that includes prevention at home and in the
community (Flannery, 1997) and in work sites (Flannery, 1995).
Interested adults, especially professional counselors, may wish to
supplement the efforts for individual youths with these larger
programmatic prevention efforts for groups of children as a
whole.

This chapter outlines the process for assessing the presence of
the warning signs of youth violence and for implementing the five
basic guidelines for intervention. These should be considered as
starting points, and are not meant to make each reader a professional counselor nor to serve as a text for child rearing. The five
guidelines present some helpful suggestions based on the experiences of many parents, teachers, and counselors in successfully
addressing the issues underlying the presence of the warning signs
in children and adolescents. In the last analysis, however, they are
guidelines, and some part of a guideline may not be helpful with
some aspect of a specific child's need. In these cases, that aspect of
the guideline may need to be rejected or modified. Ultimately, it

is the individual parent or care giver who is responsible for the child, and the parent or care giver's judgment in specific instances should take precedence.

Table 1. The Continuum of Warning Signs

Early Warning Signs	Biological Markers
	Disrupted Attachments: Disruptions in Family Unit, Dysfunctional Family Unit, Absence of Peer Group, Disrupted Relationships at School or in Neighborhood
	Disruptions in Reasonable Mastery: Deficiencies in Personal Growth, Interpersonal Growth, Academics
	Disruptions in Meaning: Disavows Prosocial Values, Disregard for Others
Serious Warning Signs	Depression (with Suicidal Thinking)
	Substance Abuse
	Posttraumatic Stress Disorder
Urgent Warning Signs	Conduct Disorder

GUIDELINES FOR ASSESSING AND RESOLVING THE WARNING SIGNS

Assessment: The General Process

Table 1 presents a summary of the early, serious, and urgent warning signs. The key to the assessment procedure is to identify potential warning signs, to note the level of severity of the warning signs, and to infer what the normal development process is that has gone awry and that needs to be corrected.

For example, children of divorce have disrupted attachments in the basic family unit. Children of alcoholics also have disrupted attachments because of dysfunctional family units. Suicidal children are depressed, and may have untreated PTSD and substance abuse. Children who disregard the worth of others have not had an attachment figure to teach them more prosocial values. In general, the clearer our understanding of what is causing the warning signs, the easier it will be for us to identify the needed resources to remedy the problem.

The assessment of the child's needs can be conducted in a variety of ways. The child's self-report of how he or she feels can be a first step. However, since children are sometimes inaccurate in their self-evaluations, other pieces of information may be needed to confirm the child's actual state. These indicators may come from knowing the youngster's personal life history, from observations by others and oneself, and from behavioral indicators that might include interpersonal skills, poor grades, and the formal warning signs that have been noted. In some cases, there may be information from medical and psychological tests. These pieces of information are especially important, if the observations are of sudden changes such as in grades, peer group, or boyfriend/girlfriend relationships. Sudden changes may indicate a recent event that has left the child overwhelmed.

When this information has raised the concern of the adult, the next step is to raise the issue tactfully. Families differ in their sense of values and sense of privacy, and schools and counselors themselves also have a number of different cultures and policies. Basic questions need to be considered by the parent, teacher, counselor, or other care giver. Whom can I trust with my concerns? Who would be an objective person to evaluate my observations? If my observations are correct, who would be the best person to begin to help me gather resources to address the child's need(s)? Who would be the best person to approach the child in time? The parent? The teacher? The pediatrician? A clergy person? Care should be taken not to place the child in the middle of competing authorities and not to let the child play one adult off against the other.

If the presence of the warning signs is confirmed, then the adults involved need to infer as best they can the probable developmental cause for the warning sign, and to begin to reflect on what resources will be needed to help the youngster. If several adults are involved (e.g., parent, teacher, and school guidance counselor for a child in a poor peer-group situation), one person needs to be identified as the person who will be the primary individual to form a secure attachment with the child in addressing this issue.

Various strategies and resources for assistance need to be considered. Since child rearing, as noted, is a complex matter, most strategies to address the underlying issues behind the warning signs will involve several components. Chapter 5 outlines the various factors associated with youth violence, and Chapter 6 summarizes the basic components of the normal developmental processes of mastery, attachments, and meaning. The information in these chapters can serve as suggestions for what may be needed to correct the problems. These resources need to be prioritized and adapted to the specific circumstances of the child. For example, the adults may agree on the need to provide access to a peer group. If a child is interested in athletics, a sports peer group might be a solution. However, if the child is interested in music, joining the school band might be a better answer.

It might be wise to consider appointing a "case manager" to oversee all the components of the child's needed resources. In health care, a case manager may or may not provide a treatment intervention, but is there to act as the patient's advocate, to see that all needed treatments are provided, and to be sure that the care givers regularly communicate with one another. Similarly, for young people at risk, one of the adults could assume the role of case manager. It may or may not be the parent or primary attachment person. In any event, the case manager assumes the administrative responsibility for seeing that the problem is corrected.

When the warning sign is confirmed, its underlying cause has been clarified, the needed resources have been gathered, and the case manager and the parent or primary person are in place, the team then needs to begin to address the warning sign in small, manageable steps so that neither the child nor the treatment team is overwhelmed and so that both parties may experience some initial success in mastery. Obvious exceptions to this general rule of approach include any crisis situations, such as a child brandishing a weapon or a child in medical or psychiatric crisis. These matters need to be attended to immediately.

General Rules

Three general rules are helpful in guiding the assessment process. The first is: the sooner, the better. Obviously, recognizing the warning signs early on lessens the suffering of the child, and hastens the return to more normal development. Many children suffer needlessly because adults dismiss the warning signs, and assume the child is in a phase and will grow out of it. Warning signs can be identified and remedied long before the child reaches the stage of violence. In a similar fashion, early warning signs should not be considered relatively benign. All warning signs have the potential for serious subsequent violent outbursts.

A second general rule is that multiple warning signs may suggest a greater risk for violence. The more signs there are, and the more severe that they are on the continuum of severity, the more likely it is that the child may be overwhelmed and may act impulsively in frustration and anger.

Finally, some warning signs and youth issues will warrant professional care. A parent may be able to help a child cope with a divorce, but it would not be reasonable to expect that parent to deal solely with an adolescent that was suicidally depressed. Not every parent, teacher, or counselor is expected to excel in all matters, and professional resources should be considered when they are needed.

INTERVENTION

General Considerations

Below are five basic guidelines to assist counselors, teachers, and parents who are attempting to take steps to prevent youth violence. These guidelines are those that have been found to be the most helpful for the greatest number of children and teenagers. They are arranged in general order of importance, and the individual(s) who is providing assistance may find that several guidelines may need to be utilized at once. With the exception of the first step, safety, the parent or care giver should assume flexibility among these guidelines, and design the needed intervention to the specific needs of the child.

These guidelines are based on restoring, reinstituting, or creating for the first time the normal components of growth and development in the child where they have been disrupted. They also address the various aspects of the anomic cycle of violence that we have spoken of, the cycle with its disrupted social fabric in an era that emphasizes material goods and may lead to depression, anger, substance abuse, and violence in many of our youth. These five guidelines listed below have been designed to address societal needs in this general anomic social climate as well as the needs of specific individual children.

Child development is complicated, and these steps will take time to be successfully implemented. Expect resistance. The various warning signs in Table 1 are the result of the child's trust being disrupted in some fundamental way. From the child's perspective, there is no reason to be eager to trust the adult world again and to face possible further harm or rejection. However, with patience, the team as a whole will succeed over time, since most warning signs are reversible. This is especially true for the early warning signs. The biological markers that may cause some of these disruptions are addressed in the fourth guideline.

THE BASIC GUIDELINES

1. Safety First

Preventing actual, immediate violence is the first step to ensure the safety of other children and adults, and the safety of the youth assailant. There are a range of possible unsafe situations. Some of the more common issues and suggestions for possible intervention are briefly outlined here. It is the primary responsibility of the adults confronting these safety matters to do what they feel is best, and their best judgment in a specific instance should always come first.

Actual Use of Weapon. If the child is out of control and is using a weapon or threatening to use one, seek the physical safety of everyone first. Put other children and adults in the immediate area under cover. Alert possible innocent bystanders, and call the police. Rushing the child or trying to talk the child down are actions fraught with danger, but are sometimes considered in the most extreme and extenuating circumstances. Little is gained if the adult is killed or seriously wounded, and the rampage continues.

Coma or Serious Medical Injury. In the aftermath of youth violence, some children may need emergency medical attention. This may also occur in acts of attempted suicide that include slashing, gun shots, or overdosing on prescription medicines or street drugs. Call for emergency medical services. In the interim, staunch any profuse bleeding, and perform cardiopulmonary resuscitation (CPR) and first aid if you have been trained to do so and if they are needed. Gather information on the type of injury or the chemical agent ingested. This information may be gathered from physical evidence at the scene, such as drug paraphernalia, or from other observers, such as members of a peer group. Since many of these situations are crime scenes, try not to touch the possible evidence, but note where it is so that the emergency medical technicians can be apprised of the possible cause of the injury or coma. The police will handle the evidence when they arrive on scene.

Acute Suicidal Thoughts or Plans. If you believe that a child may have suicidal thoughts or plans, the following general questions may be helpful in gathering initial information for medical or counseling personnel. Ask if the child wants to kill him- or herself. If the answer is yes, then get the child to a local hospital emergency room immediately and do not leave the child alone in the interim. If the child answers no to the first question, proceed to the second question. Does the child have a plan? Here, the adult is listening for a well-formulated plan. The child who reports a fully loaded revolver in his school locker has a more thought-out plan than a child who says he will think of something when the time comes. Well-formulated plans should be taken seriously, and immediate assistance should be sought. If the child answers no to the first two questions, a third question is asked: What keeps you alive? Here, the adult wants to assess the support network of the child and the child's reasons to live. A statement such as "my parents really care and I'm on the baseball team" indicate greater support than "only my cat loves me."

Always take any statements of suicidal thoughts or plans seriously, and have them evaluated immediately by professional counselors and other medical personnel. Better to be conservative and wrong and have the child alive than to be less conservative and correct, and have the child dead. If it turns out that the statements were a gesture for attention, the emergency room personnel will help you find counseling assistance. Make your evaluation based on what the child is saying, not on how distressed the child may or may not appear. Some children and adolescents who have decided to kill themselves are relieved to have reached the decision and are very calm in their last hours. Finally, when asking the initial questions, the child's answers may be further compromised and less accurate if the child has been abusing drugs or alcohol.

Assault. If a child is combative and actually out of control, seek safety for yourself and others, and call the police or school security. If the child displays the indicators of impending loss of control, but is still in tenuous control, the adult may want to talk the child down. Stand back seven feet, try to identify the child's perceived grievance, tell the child that you have sent for help, and try to ally yourself with the child's perceived injustice in terms of trying to get that matter addressed. Keep the child talking until help arrives. Then do what you can to see that the child's issue is addressed. Should the child report the presence of a weapon during this process, ask the child to place the weapon in a neutral third corner. Do not reach for it as the child may have a second concealed weapon.

Rape. Children and adults who are victims of rape at the hands of other youth need to do what is needed for survival. Various strategies can be considered, but no strategy works in every case, and the presence of a weapon further complicates what can be done safely. Some victims stall for time, others yell, some run away. Still others vomit, pick their noses, or act crazy. In any case, the victim should try to get a clear description of the assailant for police.

Robbery. If a child or adult is being robbed by a young person, the victim should not resist. Give what is asked and do not try to hold something back. Victims who have turned over their wallets but kept several dollars in another pocket have been shot by youths who perceive this as an insult to their authority. Material goods may be replaced. A victim's life cannot.

The one exception to offering no resistance in robberies occurs in those instances where the person is being taken hostage. In these cases, every reasonable attempt should be made to resist and flee. Again, the presence of a weapon complicates the decisions that need to be made in these cases.

Domestic Violence. Since domestic violence occurs within the privacy of the home, it is harder to detect. If violence is overheard occurring in an apartment or a house, the police should be called. Some state governments also have 800 numbers where citizens can report their concerns anonymously.

Sexual abuse in the absence of overt physical injuries and the symptoms of PTSD is hard to assess. However, there are often observable signs of physical abuse of children. These may include bruises on the facial cheeks or body, unusual marks on the body, burns, a distended stomach, frequent accidents, or unusually aggressive or socially isolated behaviors. Children who are observed to be hitting others have frequently been direct victims of, or witnesses to, physical abuse by others.

School Safety. Crisis prevention through environmental design can be implemented in school systems. Here, the superintendent or principal may want to consider the following. School systems have reported success with metal detectors, police presence, dogs that sniff lockers periodically, penalties for weapons possession, courses on antiviolence strategies, verbal-conflict resolution methods, and adults on alert in the building. In some systems, background investigations of staff and teachers have also been included.

When the safety of all has been addressed in any of these situations, the remaining four guidelines can be considered.

2. Fostering Attachments

The fundamental root cause of all of the warning signs in almost all cases is the failure of some important attachment to be formed or maintained. Thus, parents and other adults who seek to reverse the warning signs will by necessity be involved to some degree in fostering attachments with the identified youngster. Children who have experienced disruptions in attachments feel betrayed and will not easily trust again.

To address this need, it is important for the adult care giver to be a constant presence in the child's life. For trust to be restored, there must be consistent and predictable behavior on the part of the adult care giver as well as prosocial values that are stated and then incorporated in the actions of the adults who seek to be trusted.

With the backdrop for trust in place, the care giver may want to examine the child's capacities and needs for empathy, sharing, grieving, and true self-esteem. The basic components for normal development in each of these areas can be adapted to the specific needs of the child. The child may need support and training in many of these areas, since disruptions in attachments usually impact on several of these areas at the same time.

As this process continues, the care giver may also want to consider fostering helpful attachments to the child's peer group. Groups are important to children because they provide attachments outside of the home. Prosocial groups provide acceptance, preclude isolation and feelings of vulnerability, teach mastery skills by learning from others, and instill a sense of purpose.

Teachers may have a special role to play in the formation of attachments outside of the home (Weinstein, 1995). In many ways, teachers are able to function as parental substitutes for those children who may have parenting needs. Teachers have the elements of parental authority in terms of social power, wisdom, competence, and the ability to nurture children emotionally. Teachers are in a unique position to provide nonfamilial protection and support.

3. Fostering Mastery

With safety and the beginning foundations for attachments in place, the parent or primary care giver, case manager, and treatment team will next want to consider how best to restore, instill, or refine the child's mastery skills in the areas of personal growth, interpersonal growth, and academic achievement. The team will want to consider how best to teach the child the skills that he or she needs to master.

One helpful general approach is to teach the child the skills that are associated with resilient children and adults (Bloom, 1996; Flannery, 1994b, Masten and Coatsworth, 1998). These skills are associated with good physical and mental health, and a sense of well-being, and are helpful in mitigating the potential negative effects associated with life's many adversities. Resilient children and adults are rarely violent.

The skills of resilient children are those that have been spoken of throughout the book: at least one, consistent, caring attachment; reasonable mastery skills; a basic healthy lifestyle; a network of friends; and concern for the welfare of others. It is not by accident that these skills form the five basic guidelines for successful intervention in resolving the early warning signs. They are the basis of sound development.

Any needed discipline during this process should be warm, caring and firm with reasonable expectations, and with both rewards and penalties. This approach may be different from the inconsistent, harsh, or violent discipline that has marked the lives of some children, and these youngsters will need some extra time to learn the new system. They may test the limits of the new system early on to see if the discipline is in fact reasonable, consistent, and fair.

The fundamental goal in fostering mastery is to reverse the warning signs by teaching the child the skills the child will need now and in the future. It is also a good way to develop the child's sense of true self-esteem, one that is based on an accurate perception of one's strengths and weaknesses.

4. *Medical and Psychiatric Conditions*

At times, biological factors may assume greater importance in some violent outbursts. For example, at one time I was asked to conduct neuropsychological testing on a ninth grade girl. She had had excellent grades through grade eight, but then proceeded to fail grade nine three years in a row. Her angry parents were convinced that she was not studying and stood guard outside her room at night to make sure that she was doing her homework. After the third failed year, the principal ordered her not to return to school until she changed her bad attitude. The youngster alternated between states of anger and sadness, and everyone was very tense. The neuropsychological testing revealed that she had a dysgraphia, an inability to write out what she was thinking. It was suggested to the school that she be given oral exams, which had been the case through grade eight, and she passed with high grades. The anger that might have resulted in violence dissolved.

To avoid missing medical problems such as these, every child should have a full physical exam and a psychological exam that should cover the areas of neuropsychological intactness, intelligence, skills and aptitudes, and personality features. Medical problems can be ruled out, and the gathered information will be of immense value in developing remedial interventions that are fully tailored to a child's individual needs.

The parent or primary care giver and the case manager will also want to consider the child's temperament, and how specific interventions may be further tailored. For example, a sensation-seeking youngster may need many different tasks; an impulsive child may need extra learning trials for mastering frustration tolerance and delay of gratification.

Specific medical interventions may be needed for the serious warning signs of depression, substance abuse, PTSD, and for the urgent warning signs of conduct disorder. Parents, primary care givers and case managers may want to consult the child's physician or professional therapist. The advice of these specialists should always be heeded.

Depression is a medical illness, and there are a variety of ways to treat this warning sign. In cases where the depression is due primarily to loss, grieving the loss (see Guideline 5, below), and finding new direction in life after the loss can be very helpful to the child or adolescent. Talking things out, expressing anger and sadness, and starting out on new adventures can lift the depression in many youths.

In those cases, where the depression may have genetic roots or the loss has been so severe that the youngster has become biologically depressed, medicines and other medical interventions may be of great assistance in restoring the youngster's normal biological functioning and general level of energy. Grieving may be an additional needed component of care in some of these. In cases where the depressed youngster has suicidal thoughts or behaviors, a brief hospitalization in a nearby medical facility may be needed to contain the youngster's self-destructive rage. This may be especially true for a suicidally depressed teenager who is being given antidepressant medication. At some point in the first thirty days of taking the medicine, the teenager's body will become re-energized enough to act on the suicidal thoughts, but not energized enough as yet to feel that the depression has lifted. The brief hospital visit during this period helps to contain the suicidal preoccupations during this interim period until the medicine has begun to treat the depression effectively.

Since substance abuse may disinhibit cortical control, as noted, destroy general health, wreak havoc on family life, and interfere with traumatic memory recall in cases where substances are being used to self-medicate untreated PTSD, it is important that the youngster's plans for growth include a substance abuse treatment component.

In cases of long-standing addictions, a medically supervised detoxification process may need to be included. The detoxification is to remove the bulk of the offending substance from the youngster's body safely and without undue side effects.

In these and other cases where detoxification has not been needed, ongoing counseling and support are necessary until it is clear to the adult care givers that the addictive pattern of behavior has stopped. Substance abuse treatment groups can be found in many general hospitals and local mental health clinics, and in employee assistance programs at work sites, should a teenager be in the paid workforce. Alcoholics Anonymous programs listed in the local white pages offer a variety of services for addicted young people (Young People's AA), for nonaddicted adult family members (Alanon, Adult Children of Alcoholics), and for nonaddicted young family members (Alateen). Narcotics Anonymous provides similar support groups for persons addicted to the other types of drugs.

Substance abuse treatment is a fundamental treatment component in those cases where it is needed for the warning signs to be fully addressed. The substance abusing youngster may deny its importance. That is part of the illness. Parents and care givers should never underestimate the importance of treating substance abuse to prevent violence and to restore the child to a more normal life.

PTSD may also be successfully treated (Flannery, 1994a). Often these treatments are not utilized because much PTSD goes undetected, and because victims are ashamed of what has befallen them.

Again, parents and care givers can be very helpful in this regard if they recognize the warning signs of PTSD, or if they learn of actual traumatic events in the youngster's life. Again, successful treatment is built on restoring reasonable mastery, caring attachments, and a renewed meaning in life in spite of the ugliness associated with the violence in the child's life. Parents and care givers become an important first caring attachment in the recovery process. There are also steps for restoring reasonable mastery that parents and care givers can include, such as helping the victim restore a more normal daily routine, or joining in needed relaxation exercises to reduce the physiological arousal associated with the aftermath of traumatic events. However, even here, some victims may feel frightened and vulnerable in a relaxed state. For these, aerobic exercise (after medical clearance) may be helpful, but for those with panic disorder aerobic exercises will increase the panic attacks and soft music may be a helpful substitute. (See Flannery [1994a] for a discussion of how to choose the best form of relaxation exercises in any given case.)

At some point, the youngster will need to address the violent episode directly. This is best left in the hands of professionally trained trauma counselors. This specialist will review the facts of what has happened with the child, help the child to grieve over the event, and then help the child to develop a new meaning in life so that normal functioning is restored. It is important that the therapist be trained in the use of psychological trauma interventions, as these skills differ from those utilized in general counseling interventions. Local professional medical and counseling societies can provide the names of such trauma specialists.

Conduct disorder is usually the most difficult issue to resolve because the extent of the child's anger and violence toward self or others is so intense. These are our most troubled children, and professional assistance will almost surely be needed. There are some medicines that may help with the conduct disordered youngster's depressive and impulsive feelings, and residential placement outside of the home for a time may also be needed to provide for the child a structure that contains cognitive and behavioral disorganization. In the structured setting, the creating of needed attachments and the teaching of necessary social skills can proceed more effectively than in the community where the child may be still exposed to an antisocial peer group, a life of street crime, and a lifestyle of substance abuse.

Professionals in all disciplines are there to assist parents, teachers, counselors, and case managers in developing the best approach for a conduct disordered child.

5. *Fostering a Meaningful Purpose in Life*

The last guideline turns our attention to the child's value system and the basic attitudes that guide the child's life. The data and theories on youth violence that we have examined make a compelling case for seeking some semblance of balance between the current cultural values of primacy of self, material acquisition, and instant gratification, and the more traditional prosocial values of honesty, trustworthiness, personal responsibility, and respect for the rights of others. The Declaration of Independence, the great religions of the world, and the research on resilient children all suggest the importance of a balance between reasonable ambition and concern for the welfare of others. The research demonstrates that, even in our own age, the traditional values are best for the child's growth and success as well as for the integrity of families and communities (Bloom, 1996; Masten and Coatsworth, 1998).

Parents, teachers, and counselors can promote these values in children by direct teaching, by modeling prosocial behaviors in their own interactions with the young, and by encouraging children to volunteer to be of service to others. Visiting the elderly in a nursing home, serving meals to the homeless in a shelter, being a Big Brother or Big Sister are all examples of how children can learn from their own experience the importance of concern for others.

When faulty or negative values have been learned from previous dysfunctional attachments or life circumstances and have led to the development of the warning signs, prosocial values may be introduced in the process of grieving these previous losses.

Grieving is the five-stage process outlined in Chapter 3, and proceeds in the following steps: an acknowledgement of the fact of the loss, an expression of feelings commonly associated with loss (anger, sadness, depression, and grief), an acceptance of the fact that life is now different after the loss, and the development of a new meaningful purpose in life after the loss. It is during this latter step in the process that negative, unhelpful values can be challenged and rethought, and more prosocial values instilled.

Sometimes youngsters talk through their grief, but frequently artwork or playing with toys may also be helpful mediums of expression. For example, at one point in my practice, I was counseling an eight-year-old boy who had been physically and sexually abused by both parents. He was an angry young boy at home, at school, and in my clinic office. He would come in, run around the room, jump on the chairs, and try to eat the contents in my waste basket. He could not or would not talk about the abuse, so I chose toys as a way of helping him to express his anger in more focused ways and to begin to challenge his attitude that the world was a totally dangerous place.

We played cowboys and Indians with little toy representations. He chose to be the cowboys who were the good guys, and I was assigned to be the hostile Indians. After several episodes of losing, through the medium of the toys, I introduced one of the Indians as the medicine man, a doctor who helped the other Indians get better. I would patch up my wounded Indians who would live to fight another day. After a few more skirmishes, the youngster wanted a medicine man doctor for his cowboys. This was easily arranged, and now the child had at least one symbolic adult who could help him. In time, we were able to discuss the horror of his abuse and he was able to learn that not all adults were mean and destructive.

With these five guidelines incorporated as needed into the intervention program for a troubled young person, the parent, teacher, counselor, the case manager, and the entire adult care giving team have put in place the necessary structures and processes to resolve the warning signs. What is needed now is patience, time, and repeated learning trials until the child or teenager has mastered these steps, resolved the warning signs, and is ready to move on in life.

PREVENTING YOUTH VIOLENCE: SOME FINAL THOUGHTS

This book began by noting that youth violence was a national public health epidemic, and certainly the statistics on youth violence are both chilling and depressing in confirming the types and extent of these acts. For some of us, the headlines of youth violence in schools and communities make us understand the seriousness of this matter. For others of us, there are personal experiences with violence among the young that impress upon us the extent of this epidemic.

In the two years that I was doing the basic research for this book, three of my colleagues had one of their children murdered by another young person. Three boys cut down in the springtime of their lives. Three other young males who will probably spend their lives in jail. Six families whose lives will be forever shattered. My colleagues were good hardworking people who spent long hours attentive to the task of child rearing. They reared good children with good values, and the future was promising for each child, for the parents, and for society as a whole. In three instants, each was gone forever. These deaths did not make national headlines, but they are part of our national epidemic. What is equally distressing is that my personal experience is not dissimilar from that of many other children and adults. The national epidemic is enveloping all of us. One by one. Event by event.

We have reviewed the extent of youth violence, its various causes, and the concept of the anomic cycle of violence as a way of having some general understanding of what is happening to our children in this era of intense, postindustrial, social change. We have considered the continuum of early, serious, and urgent warning signs, and how they are placed in order of increasing severity to illustrate how unattended early warning signs become worse over time. The warning signs are many and recognizable, and have often been there for several years. Finally, we reviewed the basic guidelines to remedy these issues and to restore our young people to more normal growth and development.

Rearing children, as we have seen, is difficult. It requires time, love, attention, work, and money. As a nation we must find a balance between pursuing material goods and allowing the needed hours for successful child rearing. Our children are our future. They should not be an endangered species. With the collective efforts of parents, teachers, and counselors, youth violence need not be the war that never ends.

(Flannery, R. B., Jr. *Preventing Youth Violence: A Guide for Parents, Teachers, and Counselors*. Riverdale, NY: American Mental Health Foundation, 2012. Chapter 6.)

SIX

Recovery: Help for Victims

Hello darkness, my old friend.
—PAUL SIMON

Remember in the depth and even agony of despondency that you will feel well again.
—ABRAHAM LINCOLN

Mrs. Ellis walked slowly from the Senior Citizen Center luncheon toward her apartment. The air was clear and crisp. The mountains in the distance retained their snowy crowns as the aspens turned their golden hue of yellow. Her Benjamin had brought her to these mountains several decades before and she had grown to love them both.

Benjamin's illness in the forty-ninth year of their marriage had been particularly difficult for her. In spite of her own poor health, she had kept him at home during those years of his failing health so that he could die in her arms. The instant of his death had shattered her soul for almost two years and her widowhood had been yet another study in how loneliness ages the human heart.

Their life had been difficult. Money had always been scarce in those early years. To carry to term their only child she had had to lie flat in bed for the last seven months of the pregnancy. But love could make it easy, and they had striven for perfect love. Gradually they put the pieces together, raised their daughter Carolyn whom they deeply loved, and helped others in need as best they could.

She reached for the key and unlocked the door to her apartment. Suddenly she felt a sharp sting on her left cheekbone. A second blow to her neck followed. She fell forward on the scatter rug, hit her skull on the corner of the table when she lost her balance, and now lay bleeding on the floor. Her hearing aid had been jarred loose.

The assailant came at her again from behind. Verbal epithets of loathing and disgust were followed by several blows to her lower spine. The assailant kicked her over onto her back, and Mrs. Ellis saw such hatred in the perpetrator's eyes. Repeated kicks left Mrs. Ellis unconscious.

The police questioned her in the emergency room. Did she know her assailant? No. My eyes were bloodied. Could she give a description? No. I was attacked from behind. The police left. She began to cry quietly. Mrs. Ellis did know her assailant. It was her daughter Carolyn.

Mrs. Ellis's experiences illustrate an increasing form of violence in our culture, that of elder abuse by one's own children. General frustration at one's lot in life, the search for an early inheritance to sustain the good life, and anger at the responsibility for an older adult in failing health are some of the reasons adult children abuse their parents. None of it is acceptable behavior, and in each case the parental victim may well develop post-traumatic stress disorder. We cannot assume that elderly persons are better able to cope with traumatic events because they have experienced other painful events over a period of many years. The sense of being overwhelmed and out of control, the sense of betrayal by a loved one, the sense of the utter futility of such violence are as intense for older persons as they would be for any of us at any age.

But life continues for all victims, including the elderly, and Mrs. Ellis must now ask herself the basic questions that each victim confronts: What happens to me next? How do I go on? How do I put these painful memories behind me? What must I do to feel better? These are important questions for those of you who are victims, and we turn our attention now to the goals and treatment steps on the path to recovery.

RECOVERING FROM POSTTRAUMATIC STRESS DISORDER

The Goals

As a victim, you have been dealt with unfairly by life's fortunes. You deserve, and you will want, to utilize the best strategies for coping with your adversity that you can find. A basic theme in this book has been an emphasis on the importance of the skills of stress-resistant persons (Flannery, 2003). These men and women use their effective problem-solving skills to maintain good physical health and a sense of well-being. As we noted earlier, their emphasis on reasonable mastery, caring attachments, and a meaningful purpose in life helps them buffer the stressful events of life, including the severe life stress of traumatic events.

Each of you who is a victim of violence will want to develop the skills of stress-resistant persons so that you may use them to hasten your recovery from PTSD, and then have them at the ready as you face other more common stressful situations. Both the goals and treatment steps for recovery are based on the importance of developing stress-resistance.

There are four goals for recovery that we need to be concerned with.

(1) Reduced Physiological Arousal. The first goal is to restore your body chemistry to as near normal a state as it was before the traumatic occurrence. As time permits, you want to reduce any undue emergency mobilization reactions and avoid any unnecessary kindling phenomena that can lead to hypervigilance, sleep disturbance, and the like. You do not want recurring intrusive episodes nor the depression that may result in the chronic PTSD. Finally, you do not want the continuous endorphin opiate-like withdrawal that can lead to some addictions. For all of these reasons, reducing the arousal states associated with violence is the first goal of recovery.

(2) Reasonable Mastery. The second goal should be the presence of some sense of reasonable mastery. You want to be able to exert

some personal control over the daily events in your life, and to be able to press on in life without being interrupted by intrusive memories or having to avoid people, places, and things to keep from feeling distressed and uncomfortable. No victim wants to feel helpless in the face of the various stressful life events that happen to any of us, and you need not accept this condition either.

(3) Caring Attachments. You want to restore or make new caring attachments to others. We have noted earlier the health benefits to be attained by such support networks, especially the natural enhancement of endorphins that might be of particular importance to some victims as one way of regulating the opiate-like withdrawal problem associated with kindling. Caring attachments to others also provide any of us with the support and information that can be so helpful in a crisis. Being with others is far preferable for victims than being withdrawn and isolated.

(4) Meaningful Purpose to Life. Your last basic goal is to be able to make sense out of what has happened to you in such a way that it allows you to go on. Each of you needs to accept the fact that the event has happened, to grieve its loss, to examine how it has reshaped your life, and to find a renewed sense of purpose in life. These steps will enable you to review your fundamental beliefs, to restore order in the face of harmful events, and to ensure a helpful commitment to the future.

Based on these four goals I have outlined in clear, direct steps the various coping strategies that have proven to be effective for many victims.

The first section on treatment outlines the effective steps for coping with an acute traumatic episode (fewer than six months). These steps tell you what to do if your traumatic event happened recently, and you are still feeling overwhelmed or angered by what has happened. These coping strategies are helpful for acute PTSD.

The second section deals with the recovery needs of those of you who have entered into chronic PTSD (more than six months) and who may have also learned to be helpless. While these steps are generally similar to those for acute victims, there are important modifications for victims with longer-standing alterations in more normal biological and psychological functioning, and victims with chronic PTSD will want to pay attention to the differences. The problem of chronicity can be successfully addressed, but it usually entails a longer period of time to master the four basic goals.

The final section on treatment shifts our attention from individual steps to recovery to group methods. Groups, either self-help or professionally-run, are emerging as powerful adjuncts to the individual recovery process. There are groups for combat veterans, persons who have been sexually or physically abused, groups for ACoAs, and so forth. Groups provide victims with different and effective ideas about how to solve problems related to the traumatic event, provide mutual support, and increase self-esteem in the search for a meaningful way to make sense of what has happened.

The steps outlined here for both acute and chronic PTSD are presented in the general sequencing that seems most helpful to the greatest number of victims. There are fairly predictable stages in the recovery process (Herman, 1992), but each recovery program, ultimately, needs to be adapted to particular individual needs. Feel free to modify the sequences as you, your family, your friends, or your counselor may feel is the most helpful way for you, but do complete all of the six steps as each is necessary to help you attain the four basic goals that are central to your full recovery.

The interventions are stated simply, but it will take some time to implement them fully. Take whatever time you need. Have reasonable expectations, do things in small manageable steps, and do not become discouraged. These painful events can be put to rest.

ACUTE PTSD EPISODES

The victim's immediate response to any kind of acute traumatic event is similar to the basic process we spoke of earlier for victims of sexual abuse. The first twenty-four to seventy-two hours requires the victim to respond to the intense disorganization caused by the event. Safety must be assured and medical attention sought, If it is needed. This is followed shortly by attempts to get one's daily life back in some reasonable degree of order. The anger, fear, and sadness that are temporarily put on hold for this readjustment to one's daily routine return in the form of depression and a need to understand what happened. If these issues are left untreated for three months, the victim will move from acute PTSD to chronic PTSD. Here are the steps that can help you address your needs for recovery if you are in the crisis itself or in acute PTSD.

1. Safety First

The first step is to make sure that you are safe. No one can make a successful recovery when he or she continues to be abused. Each episode of violence re-traumatizes you, and further worsens the considerable biological and psychological disruptions that we spoke of at length in the first part of this book.

You must be physically safe first, and physically leaving the unsafe environment needs to be addressed. Should you run for safety? Should you call others for help, such as your family, the neighbors, the police? Each case must be decided individually, but physical safety is a sine qua non. You must be safe.

Seeking medical attention is next. Every victim deserves good care, and you should seek it. Medical attention may include help for any physical injuries sustained; tests for venereal disease, pregnancy, or AIDS in cases of sexual abuse; and possible psychological counseling. Hospitals and emergency rooms can be fairly intimidating places, and even though medical personnel are well-intentioned, some of their routine procedures and detailed history-taking can feel like a second episode of violence. Thus, it is best for you or a loved one to state clearly when you first arrive at the hospital that you are a victim and are feeling totally vulnerable. Family or friends can be designated to give tactful reminders of this to staff in the course of the hospital visit.

Legal assistance may also be sought during these early hours. You may want to involve the police in seeking out the assailant. You and your loved ones may also want to consider the role of legal redress in the short term (such as securing a restraining order in the case of domestic violence), or obtaining counsel and victim assistance services from the court during the course of a later trial.

There are some other practical issues that you need to be mindful of to ensure your safety. Avoid driving or operating heavy machinery, because you may have problems with sudden startle reactions, with concentration, and with intrusive memories, including sudden flashbacks. All of these factors may temporarily impair your coordination. There are other practical concerns as well. If your house was broken into during the crime, does it need to be repaired? Did the street crime involve theft, and has it left you without money to return home? Will the violence draw media attention? If so, how would you cope with this to avoid being re-traumatized when asked to recount the traumatic event in vivid detail? Such issues need to be addressed as part of the overall plan for physical safety, and taking time to do this will greatly decrease your physical distress as well as augment your sense of being in control.

The second component of safety is safety with trusted others. Trust is especially important if you are to discuss the traumatic event. When a victim has decided to disclose what has happened and to share the nature of the violence, he or she should be prepared for the whole range of human reaction from acceptance and support to anger, disbelief, and even victim-blaming. This is especially true in cases of rape, incest, and domestic battering, and this is why it is important for you to select someone whom you can truly trust. Medical personnel, mental health counselors, clergy, police, and lawyers can often be helpful. Other victims certainly understand such things. Family, loved ones, neighbors, and the larger community may be initially shocked that such an event has happened to someone they know, but in time most families become supportive of their loved one. You want to select your trusted person wisely. In the midst of the turmoil, the trusted person will be able to help you find a safe haven where you will no longer be victimized.

But how does any of us know that we can trust someone? What is trust? Is it a feeling or an attitude? Should we blindly trust someone until they disappoint us? Can you trust someone when you first meet them? There are actually useful guidelines to help us in such matters. Trust is not guesswork. The assessment of trust comes from your interaction with others, and is a function of observable behaviors and known values. Trust is composed of predictable behavior and prosocial values (see Chapter 3).

Sometimes you can predict a person's behavior, but you do not share similar prosocial values. One might tell you he/she will continue to beat you or take your money or drive to endanger. We can predict the behavior because they will do exactly what they say they will do. However, we cannot trust such a person because his or her values are at such variance with our own.

Victims understandably have great concerns about trusting others. Again, this need not be guesswork. You need to interact with a person or observe them from a distance to see if the behavior is predictable and if the values are similar. Choose someone whom you can trust to use such personal information discreetly, if at all. When you have identified someone you can trust, you can reach out for help in dealing with the episode of violence.

2. No Substance Use or Addictive Behavior

With our new awareness of the repetition compulsion and endorphin opiate-like withdrawal and their links to addictive behaviors, it is clear that all victims need to avoid the misuse and abuse of alcohol, drugs, and prescripted medicines. These addictive behaviors complicate recovery because these substances alter the already fragile brain chemistry present in the aftermath of traumatic events. For example, a victim in crisis who turns to alcohol is at increased risk for impaired reasoning, difficulties with memory, and depression. No victim wants to further compromise his or her capacity to respond effectively to the crisis at hand. Trauma plus substance abuse equals two problems to be solved. Each makes the other worse.

Similarly, the other forms of addictive behavior, such as the sexual addictions, repetitive self-mutilation and repeated sensation-seeking may equally compromise the victim's capacity to cope with violence. While brain chemistry may not be as disrupted as it is with alcohol or drugs, all addictions consume great amounts of the person's time as the addiction is pursued. This is valuable time that prevents the learning of better and more effective ways to cope, and delays the onset of recovery.

Do not use addictive behaviors as a solution to your PTSD distress. Do not let your attention be drawn away from the true and painful matter of the violence. The addiction will only provide you with very short-term relief, and the impact of the traumatic event will still be there. If you already had an addiction or incurred one as a result of your traumatic event, get help in this matter. Consider joining Alcoholics Anonymous, Narcotics Anonymous, Overeaters Anonymous, or any of the other fine self-help programs that are available. Professional counseling for addictive behavior may also be helpful. Plan to use the more adaptive ways to seek relief from the physiology of traumatic abuse that are listed in Step 5, below.

3. Restore Reasonable Mastery

We have seen how overwhelming traumatic violence disrupts your sense of personal control, and it is important for you to restore some sense of mastery as quickly as possible. When you are safe, there are immediate opportunities to do this.

You can and should be encouraged to take as much responsibility as possible for seeing that your own needs are met. Medical care; a safe place to stay; needs for clothing or money; notifying one's employer, family, and friends; debriefing medical and police personnel who may be assisting; all are opportunities for you to reassert control.

Likewise, being actively involved in planning your recovery process is another opportunity for you to establish some sense of mastery. It is helpful in these early post-trauma hours to learn about the symptoms of traumatic stress, the feelings that are commonly found in victims, how intrusions may emerge, and the importance of being with others. Such education about the potential fall-out from traumatic events can provide you with an additional sense of control during the hours after the violent episode.

A third way to restore mastery is for you to exercise control over events that have no immediate relationship to the violence. Balancing the checking account, getting the car repaired, running household errands will all help you to restore a true sense of being in control in the early days after the incident.

A fourth way to regain some sense of mastery is to avoid negative thinking, such as excessive self-blame. We noted earlier how faulty overgeneralizations (Dr. Beck) and false assumptions (Dr. Ellis) can lead to increased distress. Some common overgeneralizations in victims include all-or-nothing thinking ("Because I am a victim, my life is forever ruined," "Since I was attacked once, I can never be safe again"), and a discounting of the positive behavior ("I'm safe, but I should have had more presence of mind.") are not helpful, and you should be careful to avoid them.

Equally unhelpful are the faulty assumptions that may be universally found in victims. Common false statements include: "I am worthless because this has happened," "I am defective, unclean, and not loveable," "It is horrible that life has treated me this way. Why go on?" "I am a bad person," "If people really knew me, they would be repulsed," "I am fat and ugly," (or some other disparaging characteristic), "I am a failure," "I can never do anything right," "I must be going crazy." Statements such as these can destroy your self-esteem. While self-blame may provide some initial sense of control, over time these unchallenged negative statements may result in helplessness or the catastrophic thinking that can lead to possible panic attacks. It is best to avoid them as much as you can.

One helpful way to deal with negative thinking is talk to yourself in positive statements. With your trusted person, write out on index cards five positive statements that you can truly make about yourself (let your trusted person be the judge). When you begin to think negatively, shift this unhelpful mind-set by reading your positive statements. Counselor Rochelle Lerner (1985) has some affirmations for victims, if you want some help getting started.

A final way to restore a sense of mastery is to use the six characteristics of stress-resistant persons as you attempt to cope with the trauma. I have developed a program to teach these skills to victims who may not have mastered them as yet. The program is called Project SMART (Stress Management And Relaxation Training) (Flannery, 2003), and the specific steps on how to start your own program for yourself or with your friends may be found in Appendix A.

4. Maintaining Caring Attachments

We have seen how links to caring others improve the functioning of our cardiac and immune systems, and how such links result in endorphin enhancement. These health benefits are helpful to victims as is the support, companionship, and problem-solving assistance that such relationships offer. They provide victims with a sense of belonging and improve self-esteem.

It is very important for you to fight the urge to withdraw from others. Learn whom you can trust, using the guidelines we outlined above, and then reach out to those safe persons. Families, friends, counselors, recovered victims will all be able to help you organize your life in the trauma's aftermath. Trusted others can serve as a container for the feelings that you have and give you advice on what to do.

Victims often do not want to talk about what happened. They may be embarrassed, have feelings of shame, or just believe it will not do any good to talk. If you are one of these quiet folks, you may find the research of psychologist James Pennebaker (1990) of interest. He found that talking was good for your heart and your health. When his victims wrote or talked about what had happened to them, they felt better, thought more clearly, their blood pressure was lowered, and their immune systems functioned more effectively. Talking about your feelings of anger, betrayal, and sadness in the presence of trusted others will hasten your recovery.

5. Tone down the Emergency Mobilization Systems

It is important to remember how our bodies respond to crisis. The heart works harder, muscles tighten up, and vigilance is heightened as the body and brain become ready to respond.

All victims, including you, need to regularly pursue some strategy to reduce the physical arousal associated with traumatic events. Vigorous aerobic exercises such as jogging, swimming, or brisk walking may be helpful to you in reducing stress arousal and in enhancing endorphin functioning. In addition, avoid excess use of caffeine and nicotine. These strategies treat both the arousal state and/or the opiate-like withdrawal issue and are more effective coping strategies for you than the various addictive behaviors that we have mentioned.

Relaxation exercises may be equally helpful. They can be implemented fairly quickly and can be done unobtrusively. There are many varieties to choose from. Deep breathing or meditation, self-hypnosis, prayer, systematic muscle relaxation, viewing art, listening to soft music, and certain hobbies like photography or knitting can all be helpful ways to reduce the emergency arousal systems once the crisis has passed.

My colleagues and I in the Victims of Violence Program at the Cambridge (Massachusetts) Hospital have taught many victims to relax. Sometimes when victims first try to relax, they feel out of control and frightened. We have modified such relaxation approaches to meet these differing needs of victims so that they can relax but still retain a sense of control. These modifications can be found in Appendix B of my Project SMART, and they may be helpful to you.

Choose whichever system feels most comfortable to you, but do include some approach to reduce arousal right from the start.

6. Making Meaning of the Violence

Making some meaningful sense of traumatic events requires that you grieve the loss, have some understanding of the origins of violence, and develop a renewed sense of purpose in life. We begin with grieving.

To grieve properly, you need to acknowledge and accept the reality of what has happened. Denying or rationalizing away the event will only postpone the grief work that needs to be done. It will not go away until it is directly dealt with.

You will want to allow yourself to experience the sadness associated with the grief as you go through the stages of denial, anger, bartering, despair, and acceptance that we outlined in Chapter 2.

It is best if you share the grief with another who should listen quietly, avoid blame-making, and help to foster your expressions of anger and sadness (Kushner, 1981). Counselors may be of special help with this part. Many victims find it helpful to begin with a detailed description of the thoughts, feelings, and specific facts as best they can recall them. As you review what has happened, you may experience feelings of sadness, betrayal, depression, and the range of emotions that humans suffer in the face of loss. Reviewing the experience in detail repeatedly may be helpful for you because with each recounting your thoughts and images are more clearly pieced together, and previously dissociated thoughts and feeling may be recalled. All of this is best done in small gradual steps over time.

Mourning allows you to regain some control over the feelings of fear, anger, guilt, shame, and depression. It allows you also to explore the victim themes noted by Horowitz (1986). Themes of fear of repetition of the event, fear of one's own aggression, and the like are common. You may want to review Horowitz's list to see which may be applicable in your own case. Issues of feeling subjugated, unclean, defiled, damaged, and guilty are also common, and you need to share them with your caring person so that he or she can help you correct your distorted perception of what has happened. In reexperiencing the traumatic event in such a grieving process, you relate the event to the self now, and not to the self that was overwhelmed and out of control. It will help you to accept any permanent changes and/or losses in your life.

Some victims of violence have trouble dealing with their anger. Some have been directly threatened with death if they made a sound, others have paired anger with violent death from their own personal experience of the trauma. In many cases, victims have confused normal assertiveness with violent rage. Normal assertiveness is speaking up for your own needs and wishes in a direct, but tactful way that invites the cooperation of the other party. Rageful anger seeks its own way regardless of the rights of others. Victims who are afraid of their anger are not usually rageful people. They are afraid, however, that they may be, and that their anger may actually destroy others. If you feel this way about yourself, it is best to discuss your apprehensions with your trusted person. Anger can also be addressed in small and gradual steps. For those victims with long-standing issues of nonassertiveness that predate the traumatic occurrence, self-help groups or short-term professional counseling around this specific issue may prove helpful to you. Anger is often one of the most difficult issues for victims to master, and it may take you some time to feel comfortable with it. As cited earlier, Carol Tavris (1982) has written a thoughtful book about anger, if you want to read further.

As your mourning concludes and your traumatic event becomes reintegrated into your present sense of self, you will want to begin to explore the impact of this event on your basic values. What have you learned about violence from your encounter? What have you learned about yourself? What strengths and weaknesses did you observe in yourself? How would you cope more adaptively, if it should ever happen again? The answers to these questions will help you understand which of your values are most important to you.

With your grieving completed, you are now ready to explore the origins of traumatic violence and to find a renewed sense of purpose and meaning of life. These are complicated tasks.

The completion of these six steps will enable you to resolve your acute traumatic crisis, and to return to more normal living. It is hoped that you will be wiser for your experience, but no less impaired in your capacity to enjoy life.

CHRONIC PTSD STATES

Chronic PTSD states are episodes of abuse that were not treated initially. Victims in the chronic phase need to go through the same six steps as victims of PTSD trauma, but with the specific modifications noted below.

1. Safety First

Victims of chronic PTSD are no less in need of safety than are victims in acute situations. If you are such a victim, you should observe all of the steps noted previously in the safety step for acute victims. This includes the guidelines for trusting others and for disclosure of what has happened to you.

As a victim of chronic PTSD, you may have an important, additional problem. Some of you may be in situations where you continue to remain unsafe. Incest and physical battering are possible examples of this dilemma. If you remain in situations where such repeated violence continues to re-victimize you, full recovery is highly unlikely to occur. In such situations, you should review the guidelines for trusting others. When you are assured that you can trust someone with the secret, tell them what is happening and ask them to think through with you the best and safest means to seek a safe place. They can contact others anonymously (e.g., a lawyer, a safe family member, children's services, a women's resource center, etc.), and get further advice on what to do. Plan your route to safety carefully and follow it. To be sure this is easier said than done, but others have done it before you. Utilize small manageable steps, take your time thinking these matters through, and exercise great care when you implement your plan.

When you are safe, you should be sure to have a physical exam. Neurological and endocrinological exams should also be obtained, if your physician so advises. These exams will be helpful in determining any possible longstanding effects of the abuse. For example, if you were physically abused earlier in life, you may have sustained a head injury that has gone undetected. Good medical exams can hasten recovery.

Victims of chronic PTSD usually have long-standing issues with trusting others, and you should feel free to spend extra time studying the guidelines for trusting others, and observing the behavior of others so that the process of trusting can be gradually restored. Trusting others may be a continuing issue for you to work on.

2. No Substance Use or Addictive Behavior

Substance use and addictive behaviors complicate recovery in the ways we have noted earlier. Since many chronically abused victims have often started to self-medicate with some form of addictive behavior, sobriety or being straight is a must. If you have been addicted for a long time, it can be several months (in the case of alcohol, twelve to eighteen months) before your brain chemistry fully returns to normal. Other forms of addictive behavior besides drugs and alcohol must also be avoided. Concurrent treatment for trauma can begin when your addiction is controlled and your mind is clear. A recovery process is temporarily blocked by an addiction, so it is important to keep trying to master the addictive process. Any Alcoholics Anonymous meeting can show you that it can be done.

3. Restore Reasonable Mastery

As a victim of chronic PTSD you are subject to the same issues of loss of control as are acute victims. You too need to engage in the various steps to restore mastery that we have already noted: take control of some aspect of your life, plan your recovery, avoid the various types of negative thinking, and develop the skills of stress-resistant persons.

Because your trauma has remained untreated for a long period of time, you may have additional issues with mastery and helplessness.

The first problem is that of learned helplessness. As we have noted earlier, this stance of helplessness by its very nature may be keeping you from solving your more fundamental trauma issues. The helplessness must be treated first.

The Project SMART program has proven to be useful in this regard. When the criteria for safety and elimination of addictive behavior have been met, some helpless victims recover much more quickly if they join a Project SMART program first. The steps of the program have been written out in Appendix A. If you have developed helplessness, and participate in a Project SMART group, you will learn the characteristics of stress-resistant persons even as you begin to overcome the helplessness. You will then be able to correct what negative thinking you may have learned over the years, and then take self-initiated action in restoring your life to normal.

The second possible mastery problem for those who are victims of chronic PTSD is the development of panic attacks. Such attacks in victims may result from faulty labeling of body events as catastrophic (Hawton et al, 1989).

The best way to reduce panic attacks from trauma is to challenge your automatic faulty thinking. What is the real evidence that you are going crazy? Or are having a fatal heart attack? and so forth. Are you thinking in an all-or-nothing frame of mind? Are you really having an anxiety attack or have you mislabeled normal body processes as catastrophic events? How would someone else view what is happening to you? And what would actually happen if you did have the panic attack? You would be uncomfortable, but you would not go crazy, nor be totally out of control.

When you fear a panic attack, use a form of relaxation (not aerobic exercise), try not to be overcontrolling of the event, challenge your catastrophic thinking, and face the situation with your new perspective. In time, when you feel better, make yourself deal with issues or places that you have avoided for fear of panic attacks. Take a "safe" person with you the first few times, until you learn that nothing catastrophic is going to happen.

A long-standing history of panic attacks can be a nuisance that is hard to master on one's own, because often most every place comes to signify a possible panic attack. If you would find a counselor to be of help, there are very effective professional treatments for panic attacks. Your family physician or local health care agency should be able to provide you with a list of qualified people who can be of assistance.

4. Maintaining Caring Attachments

Victims of chronic PTSD often withdraw from the network of caring attachments that was theirs. The need for caring links to others is no less true for chronic abuse victims than for victims in acute PTSD.

Review the steps for trusting others, and some of the suggestions that were offered earlier in Step 4 for victims in the acute PTSD phase. Start in small ways. You need only to build or rebuild one attachment at a time. Rely on others in little ways at first. Gradually you will feel more safe, more relaxed, and more supported by others. Building links to others often takes longer for victims of chronic abuse, so be patient with yourself in the process.

Some victims of sexual abuse may additionally experience issues in restoring physical and psychological sexual intimacy. Counselors can be helpful with these matters, and family therapist Dr. Gina Ogden (1990) has written a useful book for victims on this special topic.

5. Tone down the Emergency Mobilization System

As a victim of longstanding abuse, you are more likely to have problems with kindling and its opiate-like withdrawal, and you should include a method of relaxation in your recovery program from the list of methods that was presented earlier. Aerobic exercises (except for victims with panic attacks) and relaxation exercises modified for victims (see Appendix B in Project SMART) may be particularly helpful for chronic arousal states. Avoid excess caffeine or nicotine. As a victim long-standing untreated states of chronic arousal, you will need to practice consistently to maintain low states of arousal.

Medicine is sometimes helpful in reducing the long-standing symptoms associated with chronic PTSD. Antianxiety medicines can be helpful for hypervigilance, sleep disturbance, and some of the other symptoms associated with physiological arousal and avoidance. Antidepressant medications can be helpful with the intrusive memories, including flashbacks, as well as panic attacks. Seek the advice of your physician in these matters if you feel medicine may be helpful. Since addictive behavior is common in chronic PTSD victims, you and your physician will want to monitor the prescribed medicines to avoid any excessive use of what your doctor has ordered. If medicines are used correctly, you need not unnecessarily fear becoming addicted again. This is a personal issue, however, and each victim must decide this matter for him- or herself.

6. Making Meaning of the Violence

To make meaningful sense of traumatic events, victims of chronic PTSD like victims of acute PTSD need to grieve the losses in their lives first. Exploring the roots of violence and searching for a new purposeful meaning in life come later.

To grieve properly, you need to go through the same steps as we noted earlier: accept the reality of the event, experience the grief, mourn the loss, accept the new limitations, and review basic values. (See Step 6 in acute situations for greater detail.)

There is one important difference, however, in cases of long-standing abuse. *The traumatic event must be grieved in small manageable steps.* This seems to fly in the face of common sense. Most victims, when they finally decide to face the event, want to do it all at once, and be done with it. *Recalling the traumatic event in vivid detail with all the painful feelings all at once is not helpful. You may be biologically re-traumatized and once again feel psychologically overwhelmed. Everything may be made worse and your recovery may be delayed. The basic strategy for grieving abuse of a chronic nature is to recall the traumatic event in the grieving process with your trusted other or counselor in small manageable steps so that each aspect of the event can be mourned, and so that its painful feelings and memories are gradually assimilated into your present self.*

For example, weekly steps might start with a discussion of where the event took place. A later discussion could include when the assailant was first noticed. This could be followed in the third week by when the victim knew he or she would be victimized. A discussion of a part of the actual trauma would follow next, and so forth, until the whole episode is recounted. This is a painful process, but it allows you to assimilate the event and any dissociated aspect of the event, fully. It allows you to experience the fear, anger, shame, guilt, and depression common to the event, and in time, to gain mastery over the event.

Since the recall of past traumatic events can be overwhelming for some victim, a brief hospitalization may prove helpful in cases where the victims feels acutely suicidal, becomes severely depressed, or needs help in containing his or her feelings. Trauma is a medical condition, and no victim should be ashamed of seeking any necessary medical care.

The medical research is unclear as to whether flashbacks and intrusive memories can ever be fully eliminated, but these six steps can markedly reduce their frequency and intensity. The research is also unclear whether every victim can recall past traumatic events in a way that is helpful to him or her. Some victims appear so overwhelmed by the recall of such episodes that in some cases it is better to leave the event sealed in memory and to work on the other steps toward a more normal life. This would leave the victim subject to possible intrusive memories in the face of threat or loss, but given our current understanding of treating these events, this may be a better solution in some few victims. Each case needs to be decided on its own merits. Since victims often want to avoid dealing with such events and memories, if you are wondering what is best for you, ask a counselor, another victim, your family, or your physician for advice.

As with victims of acute PTSD events, when you have completed your grieving process, you are now ready to explore the origins of violence and to find a new meaningful purpose in life.

The completion of these six steps will enable you to attain a more normal daily routine, and to be freed of the burden of untreated trauma that so hardens the heart. Some of you may continue to recall the event, but you will now have better control of such intrusive memories and the painful feelings that they evoke. In following these steps you will enhance your stress-resistance and attain the treatment goals of reasonable mastery, caring attachments, and begin the process of finding a meaningful purpose in life in your newly relaxed state.

GROUP TREATMENT

Groups can be very helpful additional tools for recovery for victims, in addition to victims' individual efforts to resolve such events.

Groups provide any of us with forums for acceptance. This is especially true for PTSD if the group is composed of other victims. As we noted earlier, other victims can facilitate the new member's disclosure of the violence, and can provide new ideas about how to cope with the aftermath. Such help generally precludes the development of helplessness, and restores the victim's sense of mastery.

Groups also provide a context for the development of caring attachments. Such attachments help victims to avoid shame, guilt, self-blame, and feelings of vulnerability. Groups generally focus on trust, and helping one another, and concern for the other group members provides an early beginning for a renewed sense of purpose in life.

Groups facilitate recovery and are found in two general formats: self-help groups, and professionally-led counseling groups.

In 1987, over six million Americans seventeen years of age or older belonged to some type of self-help group. There are at least two hundred different types of such groups for medical problems, the various addictions, and the range of differing traumatic events.

Such groups are very democratic. They are member-run and governed. Every member has equal rights and each member has personal experience with the main purpose for the group's existence. Ask around about such groups, read the calendar of events in your local newspaper for a listing, or check the white pages. The fee for membership is nominal, if there is any at all.

Professionally led groups can be equally helpful. In the Victims of Violence Program at the Cambridge (Massachusetts) Hospital, my colleagues have developed a three-tiered approach for the needs of sexually and physically abused victims (Koss and Harvey, 1991).

One group provides victims with support and education about what trauma is and what its untreated consequences may be. The group focuses on trust, control, support, and initial feelings of loss, anger, and guilt. A second group format consists of Project SMART groups (see Appendix B) to help victims regain reasonable mastery, develop caring attachments, and avoid helplessness. A third group level consists of concentrated work on the traumatic event itself. Traumatic events are shared, memories are recovered, and some direct control of the traumatic experience is encouraged. Goals here might include sharing the secret, improving relationships, thinking better of one's self and so forth.

Each of these three group formats are short-term interventions lasting no more than ten weeks each. Victims begin in the group most suitable for their initial needs. These groups are proving to be helpful adjuncts for individual recovery (Koss and Harvey, 1991). For victims with continuing interests in and needs for longer-term groups, most mental health agencies provide continuing survivor support groups.

Some victims are initially frightened and appalled by the thoughts of joining a group. This is understandable, as victims want to withdraw and do not want to be mistreated by others again but many victims are greatly relieved and pleasantly surprised when they see how helpful such groups can be. Groups are not for everyone, but I would again encourage you to see if a group would be helpful in your individual case.

* * *

This chapter has focused on the six steps that victims may choose to utilize to resolve the aftermath of psychological trauma: (1) safety first, (2) no substance use or addictive behavior, (3) restoring reasonable mastery, (4) maintaining caring attachments, (5) toning down the emergency mobilization systems, and (6) beginning to make meaning of the violence to lead to the four goals for recovery. With time and patience you will attain the sense of inner peace that is rightfully yours.

You need not do this alone. You can do what stress-resistant people do: reach out to others.

As we have noted repeatedly, caring attachments can be powerful resources for helping victims to recover. Not only are such attachments found in groups with other victims, but they are all around us if we care to utilize them.

(Flannery, R. B. Jr. *Posttraumatic Stress Disorder: The Victim's Guide to Healing and Recovery.* Second Edition. Riverdale, NY: American Mental Health Foundation, 2012. Chapter 8.)

SEVEN

The Assaulted Staff Action Program (ASAP)

An injury to one is the concern of all.
—KNIGHTS OF LABOR MOTTO

Speak that I may know you.
—BEN JONSON

The flash of fuchsia.

It was April 29th. He knew that because he had not slept on April 28th for the past fifteen years.

He sat quietly on the bar stool and nursed a drink. How would he handle his daughter's wedding in three days? He wondered about that. He would get to be father of the bride but once, and he wanted everything to go well. The plans were in place, but he remained apprehensive. She was both his greatest joy and his most intense dread.

It was fifteen years ago, but the flash of fuchsia was as present now as his own breath. Perhaps it was fitting that the sun never rose on the dark streets of his city.

A modest family man, Henry had spent twenty-nine years as a subway motorman beneath the streets of the city to care for his wife and to ensure that his daughter's life would be better than their own. The tedium, the stale air, the incessant noise, the monotony of almost three decades of darkness were fraught with meaning as his daughter's wedding neared.

As he sat on the stool, he thought back yet again to why they had stood at the edge. As the four car train approached the platform, several passengers were crowded too closely near the edge. The young girl in the fuchsia jacket was especially at risk. He sounded the warning horn.

In an instant, a flash of fuchsia before his windshield. Cries of horror from the platform. The hiss of pneumatic steam. Screeching brakes. The sudden shudder beneath the train's wheels as tempered steel crushed bone, cartilage, and sinew. A disquieting silence.

The head and blood of the young girl, his daughter's age, lay beside the electrified third rail . . .

The coroner termed it suicide. The transit authority gave him two days to rest.

At his request, his daughter had never worn the color fuchsia.

Three days hence would be her wedding day, but in the dark night of his soul it would always be April 28th.

Henry is an example of a victim of violence attempting to cope with the untreated psychological sequelae of this painful event. His intrusive memories; his distance from others, including his own daughter; his inability to make sense of why it happened, even fifteen years later; and his self-medication of this traumatic distress with alcohol are constant reminders of the untold tale of this sad, angry, suicidal young citizen. Was she angry with the transit system? With a culture that emphasizes material goods? We will never know, since she directed her anger toward herself, and the answers to these questions were silenced with her death. We do know, however, that Henry is still attempting to cope with her act of depression and rage.

There are many Henrys, victims of violent events, who have not received proper treatment. It is estimated that anywhere from five percent to fifteen percent of victims of various types of traumatic events (Caldwell,1992; Norris, 1992) do not receive needed care and go on to develop untreated PTSD.

As we have seen, denial and avoidance are not helpful ways to deal with the aftermath of violent events, so Henry and other victims might seek more suitable help in the form of professional counseling from individual therapists trained in the complexities of psychological trauma, or in the form of an organizational trauma response team, such as the Assaulted Staff Action Program (ASAP).

In truth, if these victims had sought assistance from an organizational trauma debriefing team before 1975, they would not have fared very well at all with their request. While systematic organizational debriefing teams are effective, as we shall see, they are a relatively recent development in the field of counseling.

Although the military had long known that some soldiers exposed to live combat might be adversely affected mentally, there were few successful treatments for psychological trauma, or "shell shock," as it was known then. An important step forward was taken with the writings of psychiatrist Eric Lindemann on the subject of grief. In Boston, in 1942, there was a terrible fire in a nightclub known as the "Coconut Grove." This fire involved enormous loss of life. In attendance were young college couples from two schools with a longstanding football rivalry. They were celebrating the annual contest between the two campuses on the night when fire broke out. It spread quickly through the dance floor, and four hundred and ninety-two lives were lost. Many were crushed in a stampede to escape through fire exits, exits which turned out to be locked.

Dr. Lindemann (1944) studied the response of these and other victims, and wrote the first paper to outline the grief syndrome as an important component of the aftermath of traumatic events. The syndrome includes marked sighing, lack of strength or energy, intense subjective distress, guilt, loss of warmth for others, possible feelings of hostility, preoccupation with death and the deceased, and sometimes taking on the appearance of traits of the deceased. These were important findings, but many years would pass before successful interventions would be developed to incorporate these findings in ways that brought relief to victims.

Emergency Services Personnel. In 1974, psychologist Jeffrey Mitchell had been observing a rapid turnover of nursing staff in a shock trauma center of a large general hospital in Baltimore. When he inquired about this matter, he was told that the nurses were leaving after several months because of the stress caused by the number of severe gunshot wounds to the head and other violent situations, which brought profoundly injured people to the center.

Was this a variant of the grief syndrome? Could anything now be done to assist these nurses and other emergency service providers encountering similar situations in their rescue work?

In seeking to answer these questions, Dr. Mitchell (1983) proposed the need for a series of systematic, comprehensive interventions, based on principles of crisis intervention. Over time, this approach has been developed by subsequent authors, and is now known as Critical Incident Stress Management (CISM; Everly and Mitchell, 1997).

Early CISM service delivery efforts focused on a group intervention known as Critical Incident Stress Debriefing (CISD; Mitchell, 1983; Mitchell and Everly, 1996). CISD is a group intervention approach in which relief personnel gather after the disaster or act of violence to review the facts, thoughts, emotions, PTSD symptoms, associated with each event as well as helpful strategies for coping with the psychological aftermath of these incidents.

The CISD approach was first used publicly during the crash of the Air Florida Flight 90 into the Fourteenth Street Bridge in Washington, D.C., in 1982. Its success in helping the on-site emergency services personnel with their personal reactions to this tragedy was quickly recognized, and has led to the development of over some 700 CISD quick-response teams worldwide.

As the general level of violence in society has increased in frequency and extent, new intervention needs have emerged. Many episodes of violence are single individual episodes that do not easily lend themselves to group intervention approaches. Other events, such as drive-by shootings of young children, impact not only emergency service providers but surviving family members as well. Over time, these emerging needs have led service providers to return to Mitchell's early concept of a multifactional approach (Mitchell, 1983), and to add additional services beyond CISD (Mitchell and Everly, 1996), such as consultations and referrals for counseling. Preliminary findings indicate the efficacy of this CISM approach for emergency services personnel and other populations (Everly and Mitchell, 1997).

Health Care Providers. During these same years, there was another group of victims whose needs were similarly being overlooked. Year after year, heath care workers in emergency rooms, acute care units, delivery rooms, and psychiatric units were continually assaulted by those patients whom they sought to serve. Many victims tried denial, the passage of time, and informal support as coping strategies. However, many remained victims of untreated PTSD (Caldwell, 1992).

In September, 1989, I was asked to consult with the senior managers of a large state mental hospital. Both the management and the unions were concerned about health care employees who were being assaulted by psychiatrically ill persons. A recent spate of unacceptable incidents challenged the hospital to seek a way to address the issue.

While I knew about the effectiveness of the CISD approach, the needs of the hospital staff were varied and complex. While some episodes of violence did disrupt entire ward units that could benefit from the CISD approach, more common were episodes of single-event violence. Further complicating matters was the fact that many of the employee victims were single parents, and, when they went home with bruises on the heads, their children became understandably frightened and did not want their parents to return to work. Still other staff had been employees in the hospital for many years and had been assaulted several times intermittently throughout their employment periods. While some attempted to remain stoic, a recent assault resulting in painful memories of earlier patient assaults was the more common outcome. Assaults in the facility were a daily and costly fact of life. Something needed to be done.

It was clear to me that no one intervention, no matter how effective in its own right, could address the differing needs of the employee victims in this facility, and led to my developing the *Assaulted Staff Action Program* (ASAP; Flannery et al, 1991).

The ASAP program (Flannery 1995, 1997, 1998; Flannery et al, 1991; Flannery et al, 1995; Flannery et al, 1996) is a voluntary peer-help, system-wide, crisis intervention approach for health care staff who are assaulted by patients. ASAP was designed to include several different types of crisis interventions for the differing types of episodes of violence noted earlier. These include individual counseling for each staff victim, a staff victims' support group, group counseling for entire ward units, employee-victim family counseling, and a referral service to professional counselors trained in treating psychological trauma, when indicated.

Research studies (Flannery, Hanson, and Penk, 1994; Flannery et al, 1995; Flannery et al, 1996) suggest that ASAP is efficacious in providing needed support to employee victims in a cost-effective manner, and appears to prevent the onset of untreated PTSD. ASAP is also associated with sharp reductions in violence in some hospital facilities, where it has been fielded.

In this chapter we shall explore the ASAP program that has been designed to deal with the aftermath of the violence that we have examined at length. First, we shall outline the ASAP program, including its rationale, its structure, and its services. Then, we shall turn our attention to the empirical findings that document the helpfulness of the approach.

In this presentation I will focus on health care settings, but, again, ASAP is easily modifiable for other settings. We now have sufficient ASAP technologies to address the needs of a variety of victims.

THE ASSAULTED STAFF ACTION PROGRAM (ASAP)

ASAP: Philosophy and Basic Assumptions

The ASAP program is predicated on several basic assumptions that are thought to lessen the psychological sequelae of assaults on employee victims and that enhance communities of compassion in the facilities where they are located. Central to this process is the concept of developing *Stress-resistant Persons* (Flannery, 1990, 1994). These persons are able to develop and maintain reasonable mastery, caring attachments, and a meaningful purpose in life, skills that are helpful in coping adequately, and skills that are frequently disrupted by traumatic events as we have noted.

Stress-resistant Persons

Over the centuries physicians have noted that some men and women, when confronted with stressful life events, cope adaptively and emerge relatively intact from these events whereas others, faced with the same events are overwhelmed and become ill. ASAP has as its goal the instilling or restoring of these adaptive skills in victims so that victims do not become overwhelmed and ill.

Whereas medicine and the behavioral sciences have focused understandable attention on illness and its treatment, less attention has been paid to the adaptive problem solvers who cope adequately and avoid frequent illness. In the 1950s, psychiatrist Lawrence Hinkle (Hinkle and Wolfe, 1958) studied working-class men and women in the telephone company in New York City. In examining patterns of sick leave, he found that more people called in sick on Mondays and Fridays than on the other days of the week. When he spoke to those on sick leave, he found that many were attempting to cope with a number of stressful life situations. Dr. Hinkle and his colleagues also noted that some employees rarely called in sick, yet, when he contacted these healthy employees, they often had as many problems as those who were out on sick leave. However, unlike those who were ill, these healthy employees exercised reasonable control over their lives (and stressful life events), and they had adequate networks of caring attachments.

The 1970s saw a second major research project to study effective adult problem-solvers conducted by psychologists Salvatore Maddi and Suzanne Kobasa (Maddi and Kobasa, 1984). Their efforts were focused on the psychological factors that would ensure good health and functioning in the senior managers of large corporations and professional groups, such as lawyers.

They identified three important factors. The first was control, or reasonable mastery over daily personal and work responsibilities. The second was commitment to something of importance to them, and the third factor was to be able to respond to change as a challenge rather than as a burden. Persons with these factors were more effective managers and professionals, and had better health as measured by a variety of outcome measures.

Having worked in a psychiatric emergency service for several years where we would see some patients very frequently and others not at all, these two research projects stirred my curiosity, particularly the questions left unanswered by these first two projects. Were the findings of adequate coping skills true for the large middle class as well as the working class (Hinkle) and the upper middle class (Maddi)? Were these skills similar for both men and women or were there important gender differences? Were people born with these skills or could they be learned?

To address these matters, I designed and fielded a research project in the 1980s that assessed the coping skills of 1,200 adult men and women over a twelve-year period (Flannery, 1990, 1994). The subjects of this study were attending college classes in the evening at the end of their work day. Most worked full-time, had family responsibilities, and attended classes two to three evenings per week. They had to drive to the university in major rush-hour traffic, and often had snacks in class for energy. Their lives reflected many of the stressful life events faced by all of us at the end of the Twentieth Century.

Some were ill and missed classes. Others had nearly perfect attendance. This seemed like an ideal group for the study of effective coping with life stress.

From among this group, my colleagues and I identified those men and women who coped effectively with stressful life events so that they avoided, for the most part, the negative impact such events could have on health and general functioning. I refer to these men and women as *Stress-resistant Persons.* Here is what we have learned.

Stress-resistant persons appear to use six strategies to cope successfully with stressful life events. These effective strategies result in better physical health, less anxiety and depression, sustained daily functioning, and a sense of well-being, and are listed in Table 1.

Table 1. Stress-resistant Persons

1. Reasonable Mastery
2. Personal Commitment to Task
3. Wise Lifestyle Choices —Few Dietary Stimulants
   —Aerobic Exercise
   —Relaxation Exercises
4. Social Support
5. Sense of Humor
6. Concern for Welfare of Others

(1) *Reasonable Mastery.* Our findings are similar to those of Drs. Hinkle, Maddi, Kobasa, and their colleagues. Men and women who take personal control of their lives have better health. They correctly identify the problem to be solved, gather information on possible solutions, develop strategies to address the matter at hand, choose a possible solution, and implement it, and then evaluate its effectiveness. They also recognize that they are not able to solve some problems, and they do not waste unnecessary energy at these tasks.

(2) *Personal Commitment to Task.* Medicine and behavioral science have known for many years that individuals need a reason to live, a purpose in life that makes them want to invest their energy each day in the world around them. This purpose may involve work, family, community, or artistic goals, and sustains these individuals, even when the going may be difficult. Persons with goals have more energy, and are better able to cope with stressful life events of any type.

(3) *Wise Lifestyle Choices.* Stress-resistant persons know that we live in a fast-paced, computer-driven world of technology, but they have not forgotten that a sound body results in a sound mind. Not surprisingly then, we found that effective problem solvers have found ways to reduce their physiological states of high arousal and overdrive. First, they reduce or eliminate the dietary stimulants of nicotine, caffeine, and refined white sugar. These stimulants can turn on the body's emergency mobilization response, even when the person is not faced with a stressful situation, and stress-resistant persons avoid them. Stress-resistant persons are also engaged in aerobic exercise at least three times a week over a seven-day period. These sessions last for twenty minutes or longer. Such exercise is good for general health, and is the most effective way to reduce the body's physiological arousal due to stress. Relaxation exercises for as little as ten minutes each day is the third wise lifestyle choice. Formal systems of relaxation and meditation can be helpful in this regard as can sitting quietly, listening to soft music, praying, knitting, or doing crossword puzzles.

(4) *Social Support.* Caring attachment to others includes powerful physiological and psychological benefits. On the physiological level, caring human contact may stabilize and strengthen heart rate, and stabilize and lower blood pressure. It may also enhance the capacity of the immune system to resist the onset of certain types of illnesses as well as stimulate endorphin circulation in the brain so that we feel better. On a psychological plane, attachments to others may provide us with needed emotional support, companionship, helpful information for problem solving, and tangible offers of money, political favors, or material goods. Stress-resistant persons intuitively understand these potential benefits and seek them out in their own lives. They are not socially isolated men and women.

(5) *Humor.* Humor helps us to see the paradoxes in life over which one has no control, and laughing itself reduces the physiology of stress. Stress-resistant persons employ a sense of humor, if they have one. If not, they spend time with those who do.

(6) *Concern for the Welfare of Others.* All of the great religions and ethical codes of the world espouse the basic responsibility of concern for the welfare of others: love one another. Even in an era that values personal entitlement and personal gain, our studies indicated that those motivated for the welfare of others enjoyed better health (Flannery, 1984).

Our research findings also enabled us to answer some of the questions that we posed earlier. The characteristics of stress-resistant persons are as accurate and helpful for the middle class as well as the other social classes. People do not appear to be born with these skills, but rather to learn them over time. Lastly, although men and women may express these characteristics in somewhat differing ways, there appear to be no inherent gender differences.

We also realized that stress-resistant persons used these six characteristics to ensure proper functioning in the three basic domains necessary for proper health and functioning; mastery, attachment, and meaning. They used the characteristics of reasonable mastery, wise lifestyle choices, and a sense of humor to ensure reasonable mastery. They utilized personal commitment to a task, social support, and concern for others to strengthen caring attachments, and they also employed commitment to a task, social support, and concern for others to develop and sustain a meaningful purpose in life.

Since earlier studies had shown us that teaching the skills of stress-resistant persons was a helpful component in the recovery of trauma victims (Flannery, Perry, and Harvey, 1993) and persons with serious mental illness, many of whom are also victims of traumatic violence (Starkey, Di Leone, and Flannery, 1995), fostering the characteristics of stress-resistant persons was selected as a clinical goal for all ASAP crisis interventions.

Basic Assumptions

In addition to this basic philosophy of stress-resistance, the ASAP program is guided by six basic assumptions. We believe that:

(1) Staff members may experience a traumatic crisis as a result of patient assaults.
(2) Such violence does not "come with the turf."
(3) Employee victims are worthy of compassionate care.
(4) The episode of violence is not the deliberate fault of the employee. The employee may have made technical errors that will require further training, but these errors are different from seeking to inflict harm on the patient with deliberate intent. (These latter cases of true criminal assault are dealt with according to standard state legal procedures.)
(5) Employee victims are better able to speak about the event with peers who are at the same risk for being assaulted.
(6) Talking about the event will lead to less human suffering and more effective coping in the short-term, and will avoid long-lasting disruptions, including untreated PTSD.

ASAP: STRUCTURE

ASAP programs and their teams vary in size and composition depending on the size of the facility, the frequency of assaults, and the number of patient-care sites that are included for ASAP services. We shall focus on the basic model that has been developed for state mental hospitals and that is outlined in Table 2. This model is suitable for facilities with 150 to 400 beds, and with up to 400 direct care staff. An ASAP team for a facility of this size would require fifteen volunteer ASAP staff members and the hospital's switchboard operators.

Eleven of these ASAP volunteers constitute the first-line responders. Drawn from all disciples including clinicians, managers, and mental health workers, the first line responders provide the ASAP response and crisis intervention for each individual episode of assault. When an assault occurs, the charge nurse on the unit is required to call in the assault to the hospital switchboard. The operator summons the ASAP team member on call by page-beeper to respond to the particular episode of assault. The ASAP responder arrives on-site within fifteen minutes and offers the employee victim ASAP services. If the victim accepts, the individual crisis intervention is completed as described below. When the responder has finished, the same responder offers to call or visit the employee victim in three days, and, again, in ten days. In particularly disruptive assaults, the employee victims may also be immediately referred to the ASAP staff victims' group. In addition, first responders assess any needs for counseling for entire units and for possible employee-victim family counseling. These needs are communicated to the team leader. Every effort is made to ensure continuity of care.

First responders are on-call for twenty-four-hour periods on weekday rotations, and are on-call one weekend of every three months. In addition to individual crisis interventions, first responders attend a weekly one-hour ASAP team meeting during the weeks that they are on-call and a monthly in-service training on various aspects of PTSD and general team functioning. First responders spend an average of three hours per week on ASAP-

Table 2. ASAP Structure for Mental Hospital Setting

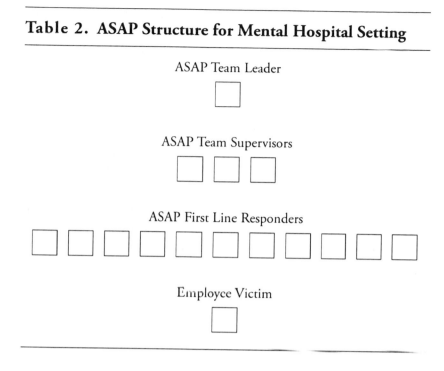

ASAP Team Leader

ASAP Team Supervisors

ASAP First Line Responders

Employee Victim

related tasks, and, as a group, spend a total of about seventy-two hours per month. One page-beeper is rotated daily.

Three additional volunteers comprise the ASAP supervisors, who are also on-call by a second page-beeper. ASAP supervisors do not provide traditional clinical or administrative supervision. In ASAP they provide second opinions to first line responders, when needed; perform individual crisis interventions in cases of multiple assaults at the same time; and conduct ward debriefings for entire patient-care units. The supervisors attend all weekly team meetings as well as the monthly in-service programs. ASAP supervisors are often senior nurse supervisors or senior staff development personnel. This allows for informal outreach to victims who have both accepted and declined ASAP services, and for the indirect assessment of needs for further staff training in patient-care issues related to violence. Supervisors rotate coverage weekly, and spend about ten hours each week on ASAP tasks for a supervisory total of about forty hours per month. A second page-beeper is rotated weekly.

The final volunteer is the ASAP team leader(s) who is charged with administering the program and monitoring its overall quality. The team leader co-chairs a weekly staff victims' support group, and co-leads CISD unit debriefings as they are needed. Team leaders are responsible for on-call rotation coverages, for meeting weekly with the hospital switchboard operators, for conducting weekly ASAP team meetings to review all cases, for training new team members, for providing monthly in-service training, and for keeping track of the paper work and requisite data collection needed to ensure proper team functioning.

The team leader has a special role in monitoring the ASAP team members for vicarious traumatization which can arise from exposure to the impact of violent events in the course of conducting debriefings (McCann and Pearlman, 1990), and for being the individual crisis debriefer when ASAP team members are assaulted themselves or encounter other types of traumatic events. One ASAP team member's daughter, age eight, died from sudden cardiac arrest at school, while her mother was at work. Another team member had his two best friends murdered in their home by a drug-addicted intruder. Others have sustained injuries from patient assaults (bruises, scaldings) in their non-ASAP, hospital-related duties. Being an ASAP team member does not eliminate the possibility of being a victim of violence, and the ASAP team leader is responsible for taking care of his or her own. The ASAP director spends about fifteen hours a week on the program for a monthly total of sixty hours.

The hospital's switchboard operators, although not formal members of the ASAP program, are an integral component of the ASAP service delivery system. They are debriefed regularly by the team leader, as we have noted; are included in all ASAP in-service trainings; and are present at all ASAP social gatherings.

ASAP: SERVICES

With this basic structure in place, the ASAP team is then ready to provide the basic services listed in Table 3. ASAP services emphasize the principles in military medicine of proximity, immediacy, and expectancy (Grinker and Spiegel, 1945). The employee victim is treated near the site of the assault, as quickly as possible, and with the expectation of the employee's returning to work.

Individual Crisis Intervention. When assault occurs and the charge nurse summons the ASAP team member on-call, the first line responder goes directly on-site, checks to be sure that safety and any needed medical issues have been addressed, and then reconstructs the facts of the assault. When these tasks are completed, the first responder introduces himself or herself to the employee victim, offers the ASAP intervention, and assures the employee victim of complete confidentiality, unless the employee victim reports a crime.

If the employee victim accepts the service, the first responder begins by monitoring the victim for the presence of any symptoms associated with psychological trauma as well as any disruptions in the domains of mastery, attachment, and meaning. Staff victims are encouraged to talk freely about the violent act and any negative thoughts or feelings that it may have generated. The ASAP team member listens quietly, and helps the victim reconstruct what has taken place. Should the first responder encounter an employee victim with flashbacks from previous acts of violence for which the current assault has served as a symbolic reminder, the responder calms the employee, states the fact of the victim's experience of intrusive memories to the victim, reassures the victim that the victim is on the ward unit, and assists in integrating the intrusive memories.

Table 3. ASAP Services

1. Individual Crisis Interventions
2. Group Crisis Counseling
3. Staff Victims' Support Group
4. Employee Victim Family Counseling
5. Professional Referrals

Next, the first responder attempts to develop a plan with the active input of the employee victim to return the employee to some level of pre-incident functioning that seems suitable. For example, in the area of mastery, employee victims are asked if they feel that they are able to remain on the unit; whether they would like time off the unit for record-keeping tasks; whether they would like to speak to the offending patient, when safety has been restored; and similar suggestions to restore some initial sense of control for the victim. The first responder also assesses the resources available for caring attachments networks. The ASAP member and program is one such network of attachments, and possibilities with colleagues, supervisors, family, and friends are explored. The team member then tries to help the victim make some initial sense of what happened. Perhaps the patient was not on medication, or had a difficult time at the patient's day program. ASAP team members are especially alert for victim self-blaming and victim-blaming by others, and these are dealt with directly, if they are present.

The staff victim is notified that the same team member will call in three days, and again in ten days. The victim is encouraged to remain in contact, and is given a card with the ASAP team member's name and hospital phone extension, should the staff member want to call at any time. All employee victims, including those who decline ASAP, are given written information in handout format on psychological trauma, practical suggestions for coping, help for families, and the names and extensions of all ASAP team members.

If an assault occurs when the ASAP team member is not on-site, the first responder calls the unit and assesses the situation with the charge nurse and the employee victim. If all are in agreement that the debriefing needs to be done immediately, the ASAP team member returns to the hospital and conducts the crisis intervention. If it is deemed not urgent, the same team member makes arrangements to meet the staff victim the next day. Team members responding during off-duty hours may be given compensatory time off within the next thirty days. ASAP team members receive no financial compensation.

On rare occasions, the employee victim's injuries from the patient assault may require attention at an emergency room or other medical facility. Subject to administrative approval and staffing at the time, ASAP team members may accompany the employee victim to the medical facility and complete the ASAP debriefing there. This provides important support to a colleague, and demonstrates ASAP's commitment to the hospital community. The ASAP supervisor covers the hospital's ASAP needs, while the ASAP first responder is offsite. (A few ASAP facilities have adopted a written policy for this infrequent event.)

Finally, when the first line responder is debriefing an employee victim, the ASAP team member's colleagues on the team member's patient-care site cover for the team member during the hour that he or she is off of the unit.

If an employee victim declines the ASAP service, he or she is given a card with the first responder's name and hospital phone extension, in case the victim has a change of mind.

Group Counseling. From time to time, particularly violent events may occur on patient-care sites. For example, on one acute admissions unit a patient went into a state of rage after a family visit. He assaulted several staff, put one nurse on a window sill and threatened to push her to her death several stories below, hurled furniture indiscriminately around the unit, before being finally subdued by a phalanx of male attendants. Staff were injured, patient witnesses to this event were frightened, and the managers temporarily felt out of control. There were sharp increases in fear, anger, and various forms of behavioral disorganization.

In circumstances such as these, the ASAP program utilizes a second crisis intervention procedure, group counseling. This group process involves a review of the actual facts of the event; an update on the health status of the victims; and a focus on the thoughts, feelings, and symptoms that victims or witnesses may be experiencing. This is followed by a brief discussion of psychological trauma and its impact as well as suggestions for coping more adaptively in the coming days. It is a helpful approach because its structure presents the discussion of powerful emotions within a structured, containing format.

ASAP group interventions are conducted by the ASAP team leader and one or more of the ASAP team supervisors. Typically, this includes three separate interventions. The first is held for the unit managers on the assumption that mitigating the impact of the event here first will result in the managers' being of assistance to the rest of the unit's staff and patients in need. In addition to this session, the goals of the management team for resolving the clinical aftermath of the event are sought. Questions such as whether the violent patient is to remain on the ward, whether other patients can request a transfer, how coverage for the employee victims on leave will be covered are addressed in some detail, so that this information is available in subsequent ASAP interventions for the unit.

A second group is then conducted for the patient-care site staff. Coverage is arranged so that the staff can be released for this meeting. The group proceeds with special attention focused on their injured colleagues, and the staff's reactions to the violence. At the end of the process, the goals and decisions of the senior managers are discussed. The managers usually do not sit in on this session in order that the staff may freely express their fears and anger, including that the management failed to protect them.

A third counseling session is held for the entire ward community with management, staff, and patients present. The goal of this third intervention is to address the needs of the patient community. Our experience has been that it is difficult for persons with impaired functioning, including many who have also been victims of violence at other times in their lives, to process violent episodes on their own unit, where issues of safety are a reasonable concern. Addressing the management and staff needs first frees these employees to be supportive of patients during this third session. Depending on the level of disorganization in the patient community, these interventions are shortened and/or repeated on several occasions, until some sense of unit order and calm is restored. Group counseling can be held for all three shifts, if the circumstances of the event warrant this.

The ASAP program offers to meet with each and all of the three groups for further sessions or individual consultations, makes available written information on trauma and coping, and generally monitors the situation.

Staff Victims' Support Group. Some victims need additional ongoing, short-term support, and ASAP provides this through a staff victims' support group. Co-lead by the ASAP team leader and one ASAP supervisor, the group focuses on the issues of restoring mastery, attachment, and meaning as well as developing active strategies to cope with any remaining symptomatology. Staff victims for whom the current patient assault has led to intrusive memories of previous assaults or other types of traumatic events are referred in time for private treatment, if it is needed.

To facilitate attendance at the staff victims' group, employee victims are given staff release time to attend, and are paid their hourly wage for attendance at group sessions during off-shifts. The group is held midafternoon to make it readily available to employees on two of the hospital's three shifts.

Employee Victim Family Counseling. Occasionally, an employee assault is particularly distressing to the employee's family members. They may experience acute distress, and not want the employee to return to work. This is especially true of single-parent employees where the children may fear becoming orphans, if the parent is fatally injured at work. The active resistance of the children creates a difficult situation for the parent, who may need to return to work for needed income.

In circumstances such as these, ASAP offers family counseling services for its employee family members. These sessions can occur at the employee's home or at the hospital, and focus on restoring mastery, attachment, and meaning within the family unit. Each family member is given the opportunity to discuss fears, potential acts of further violence are put in perspective, and the family members are given practical suggestions on how to cope and restore normal family functioning. Again, this ASAP service may be repeated as often as needed, but our experience suggests that it is needed very infrequently, and then only once per assaultive episode.

Professional Referrals. When traumatic events at the hospital have served as symbolic reminders of previous episodes of non-work related violence, the ASAP program provides professional referrals to counselors who are trained in addressing the psychological aftermath of traumatic events. Each ASAP team leader has a list of trauma intervention programs and specific trauma therapists in their own geographical area.

For example, one common outcome is for an episode of patient assault to stir memories of earlier incidents of child battering or spousal battering. After the individual crisis debriefing, these employee victims are referred to the Staff Victims' Support Group, and, at times, individual sessions with the ASAP team leader. These meetings are intended to provide support to the employee, to address any sense of shame that may be experienced by the employee, and to provide a gentle transition to the private counselor or specialized trauma program.

All ASAP interventions are fully confidential, unless the employee victim reports a crime. (In these cases, all employees are governed by state regulations to formally report such violations.) ASAP records do not become part of any medical record, any personnel record, nor any employee performance review appraisal. All ASAP records are kept within the ASAP program in a locked cabinet that belongs to the team leader. Any employee wishing his or her ASAP report forwarded to a third party, such as the family physician or Industrial Accident Claims Board, meets with the team leader, reviews the ASAP records with the ASAP team leader, and signs an ASAP release of information form. The employee victim's records are then forwarded as requested. Informed consent is obtained from all employees, and data are collected on all episodes of assault. The team leader codes this data, which is collected only in the aggregate. The data is used only for the general purposes of quality management and to increase our understanding of violence and how to address it.

Finally, with the exception of private individual counseling sessions by trauma specialists, all ASAP services are free employee benefits, and staff are encouraged by both management and unions to avail themselves of these services.

VIOLENCE IN HEALTH CARE SETTINGS:
THE ASAP RESPONSE

The Assaulted Staff Action Program in Health Care Settings

Over 2,025 ASAP team members on 45 teams in 9 states have volunteered over 2 million hours of service and have responded to 8,225 staff victims of patient assaults.

ASAP was chosen as one of ten finalists in 1996 for the American Psychiatric Association's Gold Medal Award, and has been cited in the recent guidelines for preventing violence in health care and social service agencies that have been issued by the Occupational Safety and Health Administration (OSHA, 1996). ASAP was also chosen as a Best Innovative Practice by the federal governments of Canada and the United States.

The ASAP program has had an important impact in three areas: clinical services, declines in frequency of violence, and dollar-cost savings. These findings are based on a series of research reports (Flannery et al, 1995; Flannery et al, 1996), which are summarized here.

Clinical Services. The ASAP crisis intervention procedures have provided needed support to employee victims, who most frequently experienced disrupted senses of reasonable mastery and meaningful sense of why these violent events have happened. These employee victims also frequently experienced the symptoms of hypervigilance, sleep disturbance, and intrusive memories. For most employee victims who accepted ASAP services, these disruptions and symptoms had passed within ten days. However, a full nine percent of these employee victims continued to report disruptions and symptoms for a period of months after the assault, a finding similar for reported data in other health care settings (Caldwell, 1992).

Declines in Assault. An unanticipated outcome in the original ASAP program was a sixty-three percent decline in the number of assaults over the two year period before that facility was closed. My original understanding of this serendipitous finding was that it was an artifact of the hospital's being closed. However, when ASAP was subsequently fielded in three different state mental hospitals, there was a similar forty percent decrease in the assault rate in *each* of these three facilities. (Flannery, Hanson, Penk, Goldfinger, Pastva, and Navon, 1998).

Dollar-cost Savings. ASAP programs pay for themselves. Our studies have indicated that facilities with ASAP programs have less staff turnover due to assault-related issues. Fewer assaults result in fewer medical injuries, less sick leave utilization, less Industrial

Accident Claims, less medical and legal expense, and sustained productivity.

In addition to these dollar-cost savings, ASAP programs provide a strong message of support to the workforce from management and the unions. This increases morale, and a sense of responsibility and concern for one another. In this way ASAP creates communities of compassion, a situation in which all parties involved benefit.

How Does ASAP Work? The answer to this question remains unknown at the time, and there are several ongoing research projects to assist in answering this question more fully.

In the interim, several possible explanations have been advanced. The various ASAP services appear to function in a manner similar to other crisis intervention procedures for victims of traumatic violence (Flannery, 1992, 1994). Early interventions that emphasize restoring mastery, attachment and meaning, that emphasize an assessment and monitoring of any of the symptoms associated with psychological trauma and untreated PTSD, and that discuss the event and its aftermath early on appear to contribute, in part, to a successful resolution of these matters for most employee victims. ASAP interventions focus on the here-and-now, and support the active involvement of the victim in planning and participating in the victim's recovery process, approaches known to assist victims of violence in their recoveries.

The declines in the frequency of violence are more difficult to explain. Several possible ASAP factors may be at work. First, an ASAP program supports its employees. It may be that, as they are supported, they become less tense. As the staff become less tense, the patients may become less tense, and, thus, the probability of assault decreases. ASAP permits the staff other responses to violence than that of imposing the control often associated with a ward culture of toughness (Morrison, 1989). It may be that ASAP interventions lead staff to pay more attention to the early warning signs and to utilize alternatives to restraint and seclusion, so that potential violence is de-escalated before it reaches the level of loss of control and assault. This view is similar to fixing the broken window theory in policing (Kelling and Coles,

1996), which states that correcting the first signs of trouble early on avoids more severe violence later.

ASAP may also be at work in reducing the avoidance responses to patients by staff who have had untreated PTSD from earlier episodes of assault by patients, when there was no ASAP intervention program. These ASAP interventions may free some employees from the use of avoidance symptoms, and result in the delivery of better care by employees who are no longer fearful of the patients. It may also be that ASAP in some manner transforms the work environment from a culture of toughness to one of mutual support. The arrival on-site of an ASAP team member after each episode of violence is a strong nonverbal message that violence does not come with the turf.

Some combination of these factors, or those yet to be discovered, may account for part of the beneficial outcomes that occur when an ASAP program is fielded. However, it is unlikely that ASAP by itself is the sole factor. In those facilities where violence has declined after an ASAP program has been implemented, a number of other services to address for assaultive behaviors were already present. These included patient-at-risk conferences; medication, behavioral, and forensic consultations; standardized training in nonviolent self-defense and restraint and seclusion procedures as well as ongoing staff development programs. While these services did not reduce the level of violence in and of themselves before ASAP teams were fielded, it is likely that these services in conjunction with the ASAP program resulted in these beneficial outcomes. Further research is needed, particularly in community settings, where these clinical support services may not be routinely available.

This completes our review of the essentials of an ASAP program. We have studied the rationale and conceptual framework of ASAP programs as well as their structures and services. ASAP programs exist to address the psychological aftermath of violence in health care settings and ASAP's exciting and beneficial outcomes, which are based on sound empirical research, suggest that an ASAP program is more beneficial to victims and their organization than some of the less formal approaches that we noted earlier. With today's technologies, there in no need for Ellen to be fearful of patients when she returns to work, nor for Henry, the subway motorman, to be faced with recurring flashbacks of the young girl in the fuchsia jacket, who jumped to her death in front of his train.

One of the great strengths of the ASAP approach is the flexibility of its design. ASAP programs can be adapted and modified for different types of environments where violence may be occurring once the basic steps in fielding a team are understood.

Violence doesn't need to come with the turf.

(Flannery, R. B. Jr. *The Assaulted Staff Action Program (ASAP): Coping with the Psychological Aftermath of Violence.* Riverdale, NY: American Mental Health Foundation, 2012. Chapter 2.)

About the Author

Raymond B. Flannery Jr., Ph.D., FAPM, is a licensed clinical psychologist and Fellow of the Academy of Psychosomatic Medicine. He is Associate Professor of Psychology, Department of Psychiatry (Part-Time), Harvard Medical School; and Adjunct Assistant Professor of Psychiatry, Department of Psychiatry, The University of Massachusetts Medical School.

For ten years, Dr. Flannery was Director of Training for the Massachusetts Department of Mental Health. He has lectured extensively throughout North America and Europe. He is the author of eight books (listed on the card page) and of more than 165 peer-reviewed articles in the medical and scientific journals on the topics of stress, violence, and victimization. His work has been translated into five languages.

Dr. Flannery designed and fielded the Assaulted Staff Action Program (ASAP), a voluntary, peer-help, crisis-intervention program for employee victims of violence. For twenty-five years, he has overseen the development of this program, now including 2,100 ASAP team members on 45 teams in 9 states that have responded to the needs of 8,225 staff victims. ASAP is the most widely researched crisis-intervention program in the world and has been chosen as a best innovative practice intervention by the federal governments of Canada and the United States. Dr. Flannery also designed and directed the longest, continuous study of assaultive psychiatric patients in the published literature.

In 2005, Dr. Flannery received a lifetime achievement award for excellence in crisis intervention research from the International Critical Incident Stress Foundation.

CPSIA information can be obtained
at www.ICGtesting.com
Printed in the USA
FFOW03n0017241215
19655FF